NIKON D7500 USER GUIDE

The Complete Handbook for Mastering Your Camera's Features for Stunning Photos and Videos

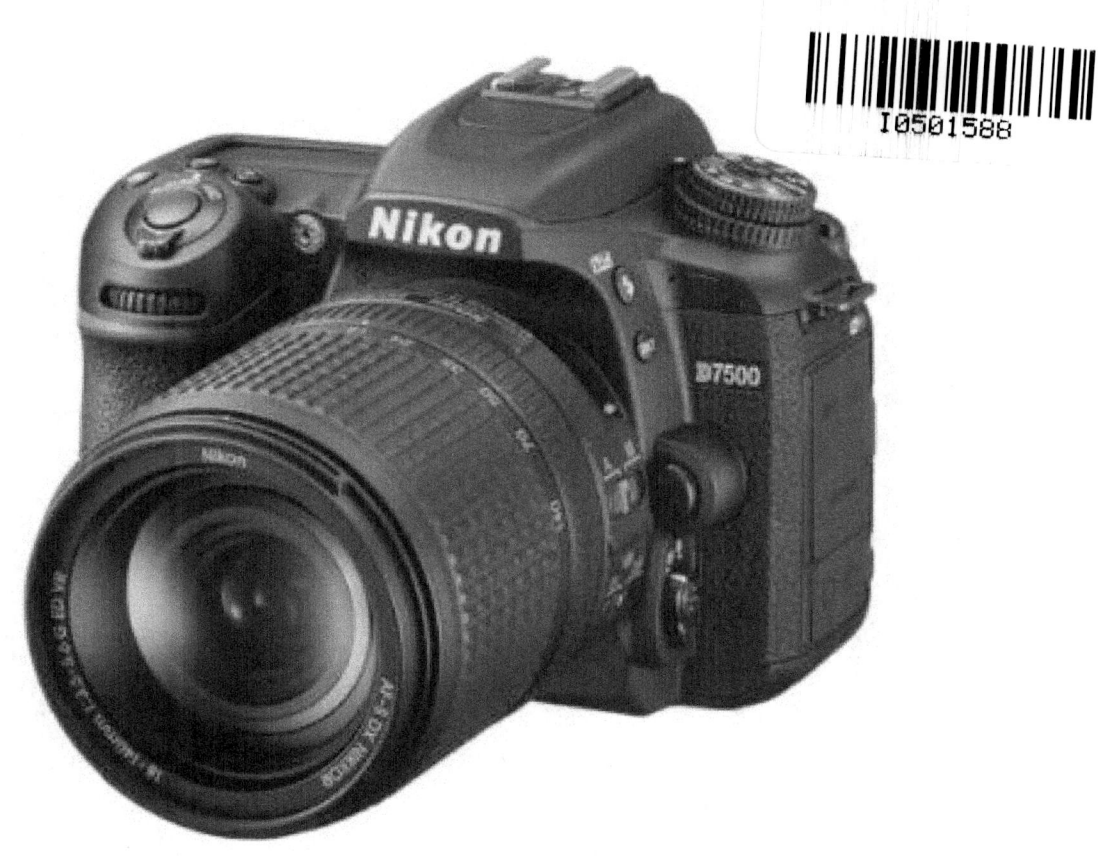

PHILLIP R. DITCH

Copyright © 2024 Phillip R. Ditch

Unauthorized reproduction, distribution, or transmission of any part of this publication in any form or by any means, including photocopying, recording, or other electronic or mechanical methods, without the prior written permission of the publisher, is prohibited.
Brief quotations may be used in critical reviews and other non-commercial uses permitted by copyright law, provided proper attribution is given.

TABLE OF CONTENTS

DISCLAIMER	4
CHAPTER ONE	6
INTRODUCTION	6
CHAPTER TWO	12
GETTING STARTED	12
CHAPTER THREE	22
BASIC OPERATIONS	22
CHAPTER FOUR	32
SHOOTING BASICS	32
CHAPTER FIVE	50
ADVANCED SHOOTING TECHNIQUES	50
CHAPTER SIX	62
VIDEO RECORDING	62
CHAPTER SEVEN	76
PLAYBACK AND EDITING	76
CHAPTER EIGHT	86
CUSTOMIZING CAMERA SETTINGS	86
CHAPTER NINE	98
CONNECTIVITY	98
CHAPTER TEN	110
ACCESSORIES AND EXPANSION	110
CHAPTER ELEVEN	116
MAINTENANCE AND TROUBLESHOOTING	116
CHAPTER TWELVE	124
APPENDICES	124

DISCLAIMER

The contents of this book are provided for informational and entertainment purposes only. The author and publisher do not make any representations or warranties regarding the accuracy, applicability, completeness, or suitability of the contents for any purpose.

The information in this book is based on the author's personal experiences, research, and opinions, and should not be considered a substitute for professional advice. Readers are advised to consult appropriate professionals regarding their specific situations.

The author and publisher are not liable for any loss, injury, or damage allegedly arising from the information or suggestions in this book. Any reliance on such information is at the reader's own risk.

The inclusion of third-party resources, websites, or references does not imply endorsement or responsibility for their content or services.

Readers are encouraged to use their own discretion and judgment when applying the information or recommendations in this book to their own lives.

All rights reserved. No part of this book may be reproduced, distributed, or transmitted in any form or by any means without the prior written permission of the publisher, except for brief quotations in critical reviews and certain other non-commercial uses permitted by copyright law.

Thank you for reading and understanding this disclaimer

CHAPTER ONE
INTRODUCTION

1.1 Overview of the Nikon D7500

The Nikon D7500 is a mid-range DSLR camera designed for photography enthusiasts and semi-professional users who seek exceptional image quality and versatility in a compact and durable body. It incorporates advanced features derived from Nikon's flagship DX-format camera, the D500, while maintaining an intuitive design and user-friendly operation.

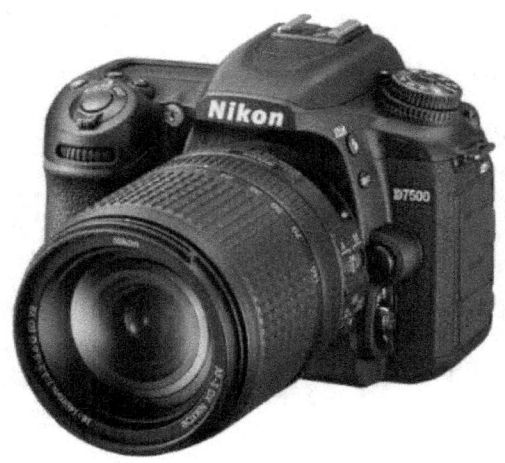

Key Features

- **20.9 Megapixel DX-Format CMOS Sensor:** Delivers high-resolution images with stunning clarity and reduced noise, even in low-light conditions.

- **EXPEED 5 Image Processor:** Enables fast performance, improved color reproduction, and efficient power consumption.

- **4K UHD Video Recording:** Captures videos in ultra-high-definition resolution with vibrant colors and sharp details.

- **51-Point Autofocus System:** Offers precise and fast focusing, even on moving subjects, with enhanced low-light performance.

- **8 Frames per Second Continuous Shooting:** Ideal for capturing fast action and fleeting moments.

- **ISO Range of 100-51,200 (Expandable to 1,640,000):** Ensures optimal performance across various lighting conditions.

- **Tilt-Angle Touchscreen LCD:** Facilitates easy framing and navigation through menus, with the ability to shoot from unique angles.

- **Built-In Wi-Fi and Bluetooth:** Allows seamless sharing of photos and videos through Nikon's SnapBridge app.

- **Weather-Sealed Body:** Protects the camera from dust and moisture, making it suitable for outdoor photography.

Design and Build

The D7500 features a durable yet lightweight monocoque design with a deep grip, ensuring comfortable handling during extended shooting sessions. The camera's weather-resistant construction makes it a reliable companion for outdoor and adventure photographers.

Who is it for?

The Nikon D7500 is perfect for:

- Enthusiast photographers upgrading from entry-level DSLRs.
- Those who need professional-level features in a portable package.
- Users who desire advanced video recording capabilities.
- Anyone looking to capture high-quality images in challenging lighting conditions.

Applications

- Portrait Photography
- Landscape and Travel Photography
- Wildlife and Sports Photography
- Videography Projects

The D7500 strikes an excellent balance between performance and convenience, making it a versatile tool for various creative endeavours. Whether you're shooting stills or videos, this camera ensures your vision comes to life with precision and vibrancy.

1.2 Package Contents

When you purchase the Nikon D7500, the box typically includes the following items:

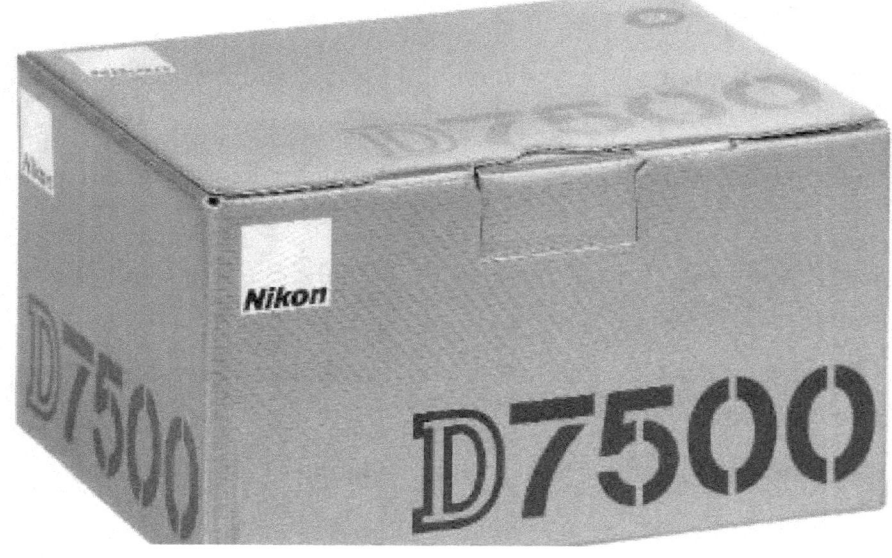

1. **Nikon D7500 Camera Body**
   - The main component of the package, featuring the durable DX-format DSLR camera.
2. **AF-S DX NIKKOR 18-140mm f/3.5-5.6G ED VR Lens (Optional)**
   - If you purchase the kit version, this versatile zoom lens is included for a wide range of shooting scenarios, from landscapes to portraits.
3. **EN-EL15a Rechargeable Li-ion Battery**
   - Provides power for the camera and is rechargeable for extended use.
4. **MH-25a Battery Charger**
   - Used to recharge the EN-EL15a battery.
5. **DK-28 Rubber Eyecup**
   - Enhances comfort and minimizes stray light entering the viewfinder during use.
6. **UC-E20 USB Cable**
   - For transferring photos and videos from the camera to a computer.
7. **AN-DC3 Strap**
   - A neck strap branded with the Nikon logo, allowing you to carry the camera securely.
8. **BF-1B Body Cap**
   - Protects the camera sensor and internal components when no lens is attached.
9. **BS-1 Accessory Shoe Cover**
   - Shields the hot shoe from dust and damage when not in use.
10. **User Manual and Quick Start Guide**
    - Provides instructions on setting up and operating the camera.
11. **Warranty Card**
    - Details the warranty period and terms of service for the camera.

Optional Accessories (Not Included in the Package)

Depending on your purchase or additional needs, you may want to consider:

- Extra EN-EL15a batteries for extended shooting.
- An external flash unit (e.g., Nikon Speedlight).
- Tripod for stable shooting.
- Memory cards (SD, SDHC, or SDXC) to store your photos and videos.
- Camera bag for storage and transport.

Make sure to check the package contents at the time of purchase to ensure all items are included. If you buy a used or refurbished unit, confirm which accessories come with the camera.

1.3 Safety Precautions

To ensure safe and proper use of the Nikon D7500, adhere to the following safety guidelines:

1. General Handling

- **Avoid Dropping:** Handle the camera carefully to prevent damage from impact. Use the provided strap to secure the camera during use.

- **Keep Away from Water and Moisture:** While the D7500 is weather-sealed, it is not waterproof. Avoid submerging it in water or exposing it to heavy rain.

- **Extreme Temperatures:** Do not expose the camera to excessive heat or cold, as it may affect its performance or cause damage.

2. Battery Use

- **Use Only Approved Batteries:** Always use Nikon's EN-EL15a rechargeable lithium-ion battery to ensure compatibility and safety.

- **Battery Handling:**
    - Avoid short-circuiting the battery by keeping it away from metal objects.
    - Do not expose the battery to fire or high temperatures.
    - Keep batteries out of reach of children.

- **Battery Charging:** Use the supplied MH-25a charger, and never leave the battery charging unattended for long periods.

3. Lens and Sensor Care

- **Avoid Direct Sunlight:** Do not point the camera lens directly at the sun for extended periods, as it can damage the sensor or cause fire.

- **Clean with Care:** Use a blower or lens cleaning cloth to remove dust. Never touch the sensor with your fingers or unapproved tools.

4. Use of Accessories

- **Only Use Compatible Accessories:** Ensure accessories like lenses, flashes, and memory cards are Nikon-approved or recommended for the D7500.

- **Hot Shoe Safety:** When using external flashes or other accessories, ensure they are securely attached to avoid damage.

5. Data and Storage

- **Memory Cards:**
    - Format memory cards in the camera before use.

- o Do not remove the memory card while the camera is on, as this can corrupt data.
- **Backup Your Data:** Regularly transfer images and videos to a computer or external storage to prevent accidental loss.

6. Electrical and Environmental Safety

- **Avoid Electric Shock:**
    - o Do not use the camera, charger, or accessories if the cables or components appear damaged.
    - o Use only the supplied charger with the correct voltage for your region.
- **Disposal of Equipment:** Dispose of batteries and electronic components in accordance with local environmental regulations.

7. Personal Safety

- **Avoid Prolonged Eye Contact:** When using the viewfinder, avoid pointing the camera at bright light sources (e.g., the sun) to prevent eye injury.
- **Care Around Children:** Keep small parts, such as the body cap or eyecup, out of reach of children to prevent choking hazards.

8. Firmware Updates

- **Update Safely:** Download firmware updates only from Nikon's official website. Follow the instructions carefully to avoid corrupting the camera's system.

By adhering to these safety precautions, you can prolong the life of your Nikon D7500 and ensure a safe and enjoyable shooting experience.

CHAPTER TWO
GETTING STARTED

2.1 Camera Body Overview

The Nikon D7500 is designed with a compact and durable body featuring an intuitive layout to provide easy access to essential controls and functions. Below is an overview of its key components:

1. Top View

- **Mode Dial:** Allows selection of shooting modes, such as Auto, P (Program), S (Shutter Priority), A (Aperture Priority), M (Manual), Scene, and Effects modes.

- **Power Switch and Shutter Release Button:** Used to turn the camera on/off and take photos.

- **ISO Button:** Quickly adjusts the ISO sensitivity.

- **Movie-Record Button:** Starts and stops video recording.

- **Exposure Compensation Button (+/-):** Adjusts exposure levels for brighter or darker images.

- **Hot Shoe:** A mount for attaching external flashes, microphones, or other accessories.

- **Control Panel:** Displays important shooting information, such as ISO, shutter speed, aperture, and battery level.

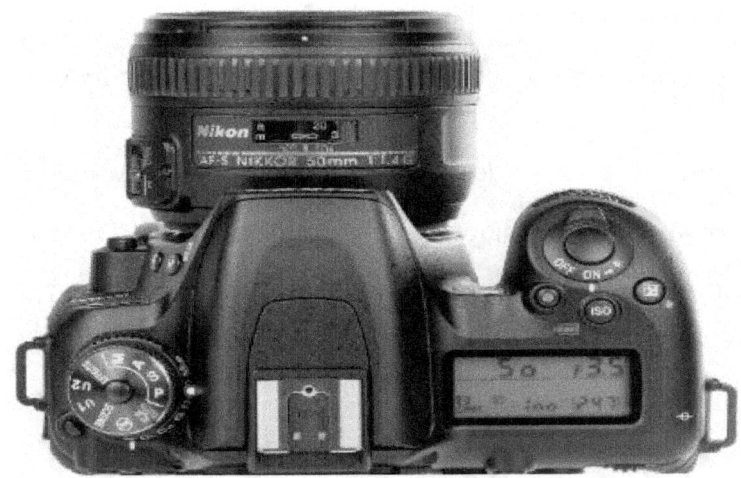

2. Front View

- **Lens Mount:** Allows you to attach compatible Nikon F-mount lenses.

- **Lens Release Button:** Press to detach the lens from the camera body.

- **Built-in Flash:** Pops up for additional lighting in low-light conditions.

- **Function Button (Fn1):** Customizable button for quick access to frequently used settings.

- **Depth-of-Field Preview Button:** Lets you preview the depth of field before capturing an image.

- **Grip:** Ergonomically designed for comfortable and secure handling.

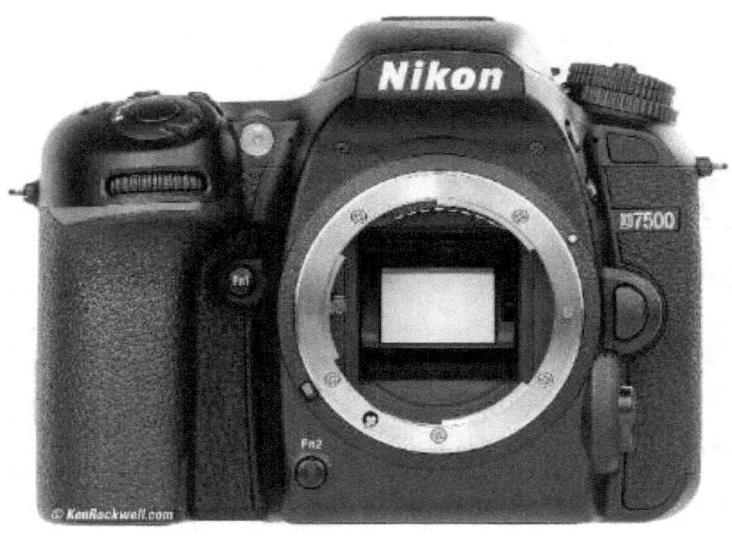

3. Back View

- **Viewfinder:** Optical pentaprism viewfinder with approximately 100% frame coverage for accurate composition.

- **Touchscreen LCD Monitor:** A 3.2-inch tilt-angle touchscreen for live view, playback, and menu navigation.

- **Menu Button:** Access the camera's main menu for settings and customization.

- **Playback Button:** View captured photos and videos.

- **Multi-Selector (Arrow Keys):** Navigate through menus, adjust focus points, or scroll through images.

- **Live View Selector:** Toggles between photo and video live view modes.

- **Info Button:** Displays or hides shooting information on the LCD screen.

- **AE-L/AF-L Button:** Locks exposure or autofocus settings.

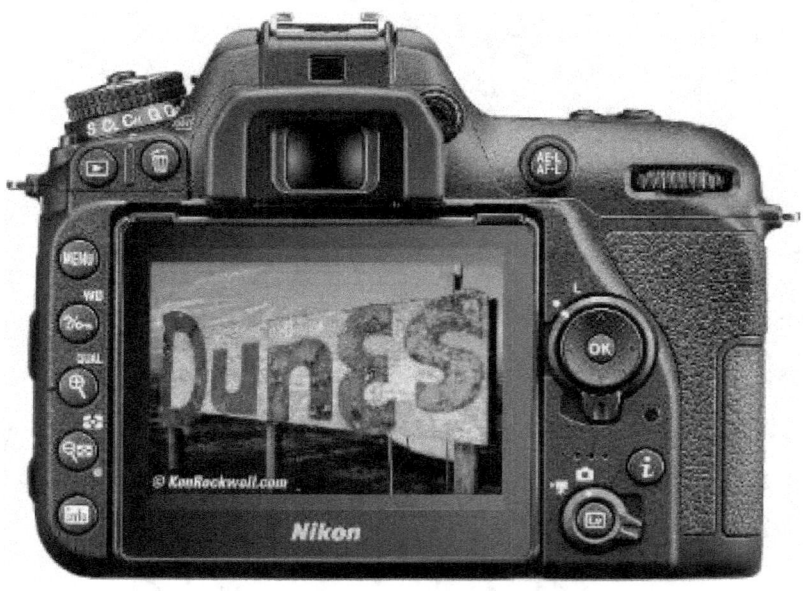

4. Side Views

- **Memory Card Slot (Right Side):** Houses a single SD card slot compatible with SD, SDHC, and SDXC memory cards.

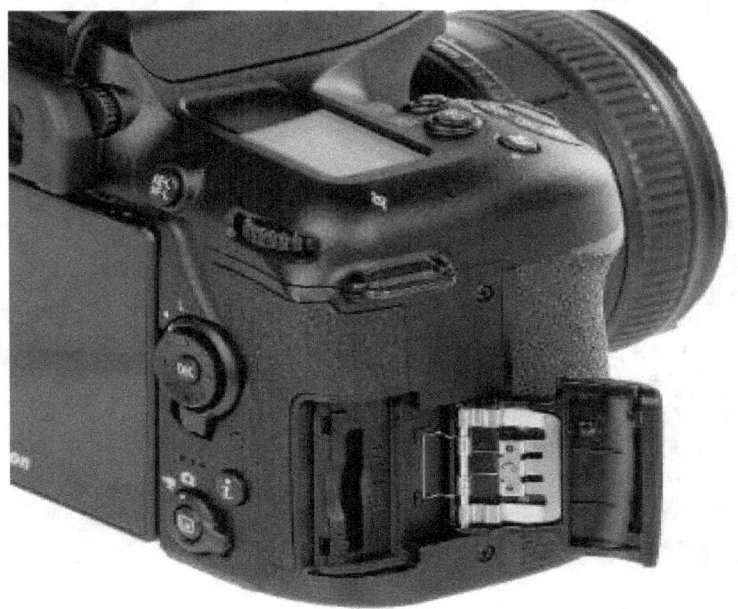

- **Connectivity Ports (Left Side):**

    - **Microphone Input:** For attaching external microphones.
    - **Headphone Jack:** For monitoring audio during video recording.
    - **HDMI Port:** For connecting the camera to external displays.
    - **USB Port:** For transferring files or remote control via a computer.

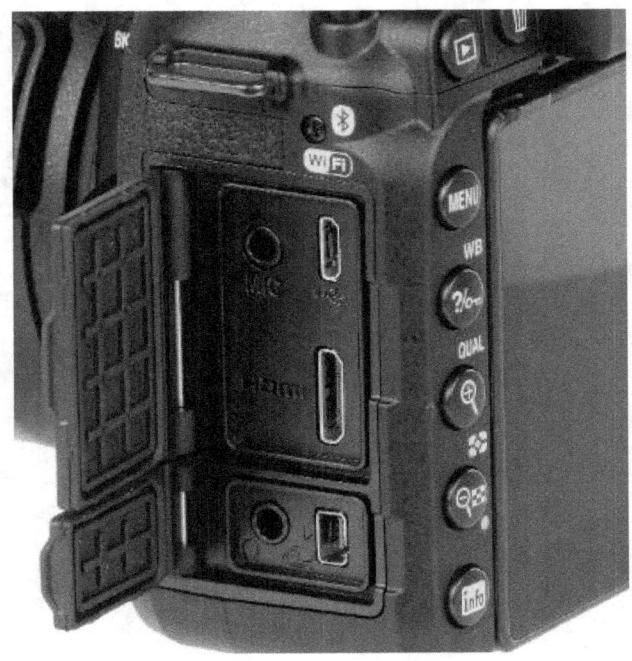

5. **Bottom View**

- **Battery Compartment:** Houses the EN-EL15a rechargeable lithium-ion battery.
- **Tripod Mount:** A standard 1/4-inch threaded mount for attaching the camera to tripods or stabilizers.

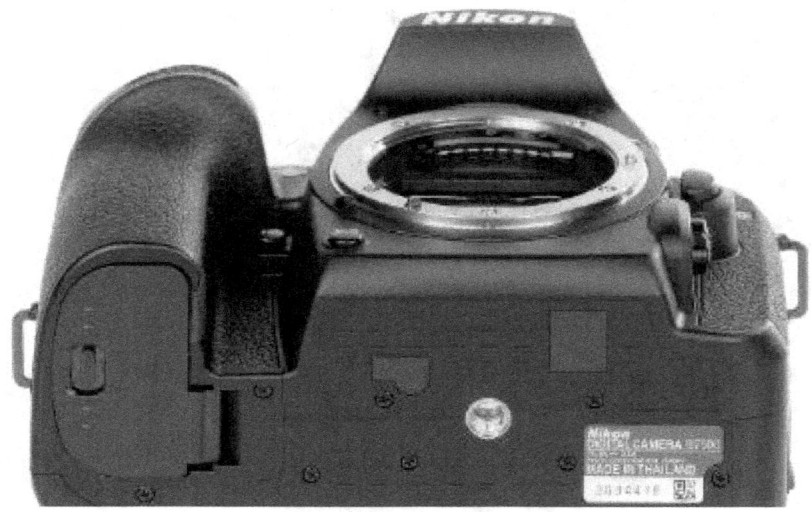

The Nikon D7500's thoughtful layout and robust design make it an excellent choice for both beginners and advanced users. Its intuitive controls and premium features ensure a smooth and efficient photography experience.

2.2 Attaching the Lens

Properly attaching a lens to your Nikon D7500 ensures optimal performance and prevents damage to the camera and lens. Follow these steps to safely attach the lens:

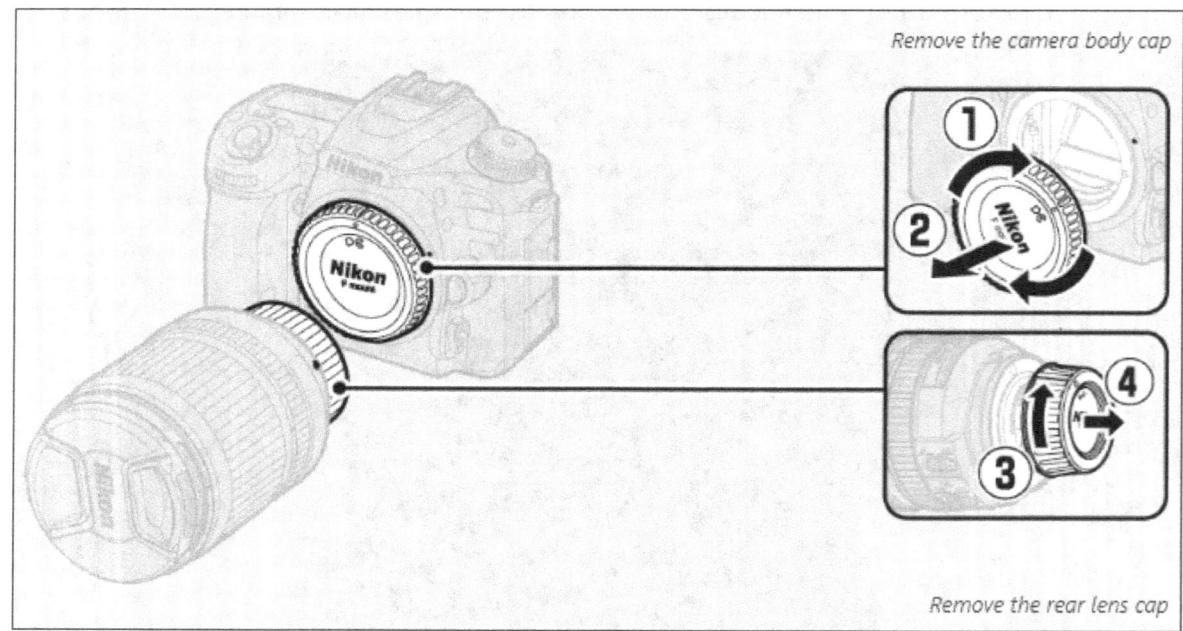

Steps to Attach the Lens

1. **Turn Off the Camera**
    - Before attaching or removing a lens, always turn off the camera to prevent potential electrical or mechanical damage.

2. **Remove the Camera Body Cap**
    - Twist the body cap on the front of the camera counterclockwise to remove it.

3. **Remove the Rear Lens Cap**
    - Remove the rear cap from the lens by rotating it counterclockwise.

4. **Align the Mounting Marks**
    - Locate the white dot on the camera's lens mount and the white dot (or sometimes a mark) on the lens.
    - Align these two marks.

5. **Attach the Lens**
    - Insert the lens into the camera's lens mount while keeping the dots aligned.
    - Gently rotate the lens clockwise until you hear a *click*. This indicates that the lens is securely locked in place.

6. **Check the Attachment**
    - Lightly twist the lens counterclockwise (without pressing the lens release button) to ensure it's securely attached.

Important Tips

- **Avoid Forcing the Lens:** If the lens doesn't attach smoothly, double-check the alignment. Forcing it may damage the lens or camera mount.
- **Protect the Contacts:** Do not touch the electronic contacts on the lens mount or inside the camera. Dirt or fingerprints may interfere with communication between the lens and camera.
- **Use Compatible Lenses:** The Nikon D7500 is compatible with Nikon F-mount lenses. Ensure your lens is designed for the DX format or full-frame FX lenses (in crop mode).

Detaching the Lens

When detaching a lens:

1. Turn off the camera.
2. Press and hold the **lens release button** (located next to the lens mount).
3. Rotate the lens counterclockwise until it detaches from the mount.
4. Replace the lens and body caps to protect the components when not in use.

By following these steps, you'll maintain the integrity of your camera and lenses while ensuring they function as intended.

2.3 Inserting the Battery and Memory Card

Before you can start using your Nikon D7500, you need to properly insert the battery and memory card. Follow the steps below to ensure both are securely and correctly installed.

1. Inserting the Battery

The Nikon D7500 uses the **EN-EL15a rechargeable lithium-ion battery**.

Steps to Insert the Battery:

1. **Turn Off the Camera**
    - Always turn off the camera before inserting or removing the battery to prevent damage.

2. **Open the Battery Compartment**
    - Locate the battery compartment at the bottom of the camera.
    - Slide the compartment latch in the direction indicated by the arrow to open the cover.

3. **Insert the Battery**
    - Align the battery so the gold contacts face the contacts inside the battery compartment.
    - Push the battery into the slot until it clicks into place.

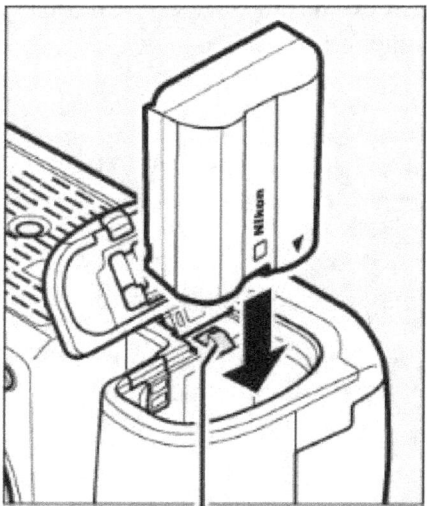

4. **Close the Battery Compartment Cover**
    - Close the cover and ensure it locks securely.

Checking Battery Level:

- Turn on the camera and check the battery icon on the control panel or LCD screen to verify the charge level.

2. Inserting the Memory Card

The Nikon D7500 supports **SD, SDHC, and SDXC memory cards**.

Steps to Insert the Memory Card:

1. **Locate the Memory Card Slot**
    - The memory card slot is on the **right side** of the camera body, behind a hinged door.
2. **Open the Memory Card Slot Cover**
    - Slide the cover outward to reveal the memory card slot.
3. **Insert the Memory Card**
    - Hold the memory card with the label facing outward (towards the back of the camera).
    - Gently push the card into the slot until it clicks into place.

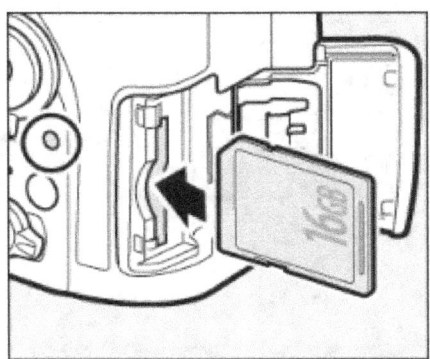

4. **Close the Cover**
    - Close the memory card slot cover and ensure it locks securely.

Important Notes on Memory Cards:

- **Formatting:** Always format new memory cards in the camera before use (found in the menu settings).
- **Card Removal:**
    - To remove the card, press it gently to release, then pull it out.
    - Avoid removing the card while the camera is powered on, as this may corrupt your data.
- **Storage Capacity:** Use high-capacity cards (SDHC or SDXC) for extended shooting, especially when recording videos.

Precautions

- **Battery Storage:** Always use Nikon-approved batteries to ensure safety and performance.
- **Memory Card Compatibility:** Check Nikon's recommendations for compatible card types and speeds to avoid errors during operation.

- **Power Management:** If you don't plan to use the camera for a long time, remove the battery to prevent discharge.

With the battery and memory card properly inserted, your Nikon D7500 is ready for use!

2.4 Adjusting the Viewfinder Focus

Proper focus adjustment in the viewfinder ensures that you see a clear and sharp image, even if your eyesight requires correction. This is achieved using the **diopter adjustment control** located next to the viewfinder.

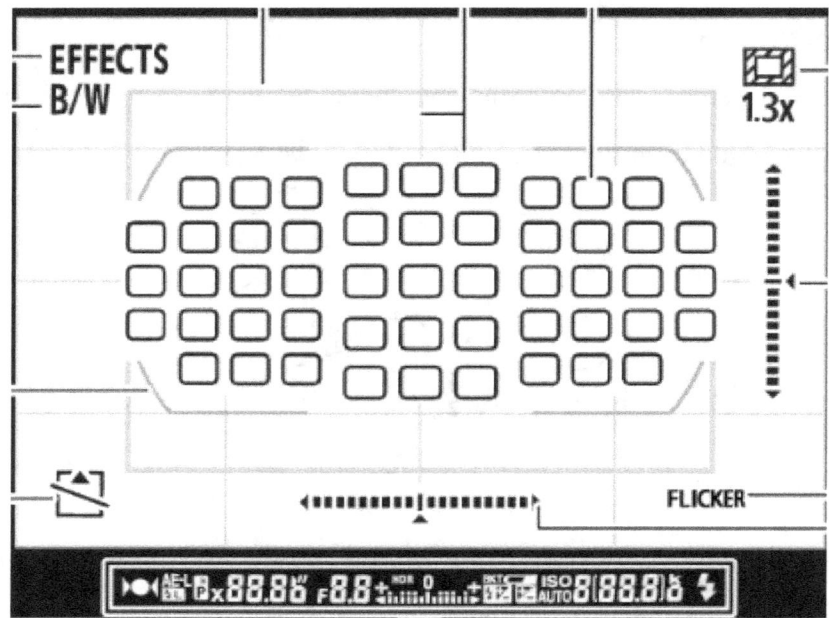

Steps to Adjust the Viewfinder Focus:

1. **Prepare the Camera**

   - **Turn On the Camera:** Ensure the camera is powered on.
   - **Set the Lens to Autofocus (AF):** Move the lens focus mode switch to **AF**.

2. **Set the Viewfinder for Adjustment**

   - **Display the Information Panel:**
     - Look through the viewfinder and press the shutter release button halfway to activate the autofocus system.
     - Alternatively, ensure that the viewfinder information (e.g., focus points, exposure settings) is visible.

3. **Adjust the Diopter**

   - **Locate the Diopter Adjustment Control:**
     - The diopter adjustment knob is positioned just to the right of the viewfinder.

- **Fine-Tune the Focus:**
  - Rotate the diopter adjustment knob left or right until the viewfinder display (focus points or information text) appears sharp and clear to your eyes.
  - Avoid focusing on the actual subject at this point—focus only on the viewfinder display elements.

4. Test and Confirm

- Aim the camera at a well-lit subject and press the shutter release button halfway to autofocus.
- Check that both the subject and the viewfinder information appear sharp.

Tips for Accurate Adjustment:

- **Wear Glasses or Contact Lenses:** If you use glasses or contacts, adjust the diopter while wearing them.
- **Lighting Conditions:** Perform this adjustment in a well-lit environment for better visibility of the viewfinder information.
- **Recheck Periodically:** Adjust the diopter as needed, especially if someone else uses the camera or if your eyesight changes.

Troubleshooting Blurry Viewfinder Display:

- If the viewfinder remains blurry after adjustment, ensure that:
  - The lens is properly attached and focused.
  - The diopter adjustment knob is not stuck or obstructed.
  - The subject is within the lens's focus range.

Proper diopter adjustment ensures a comfortable and clear shooting experience, allowing you to focus accurately and compose your shots effectively.

2.5 Powering On and Off

The Nikon D7500 is designed with a simple and convenient power system. Properly turning the camera on and off helps conserve battery life and ensures that your camera operates correctly. Here's how to power the camera on and off:

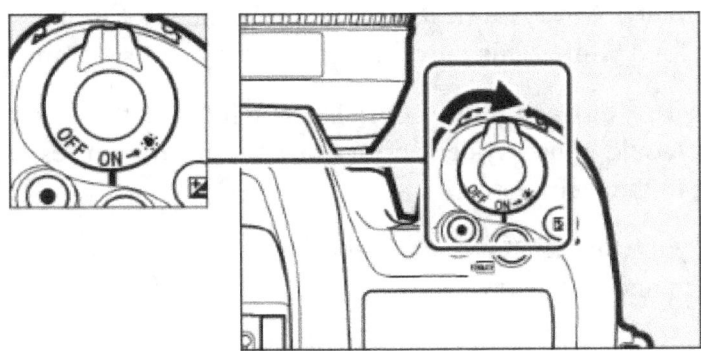

1. Powering On the Camera

Steps to Turn On:

1. **Locate the Power Switch**
   - The power switch is located on the **top right** of the camera, near the mode dial and shutter release button.

2. **Turn the Power Switch**
   - Slide the **power switch** from the **O** (off) position to the **I** (on) position.

3. **Confirm Power-On**
   - After turning the power on, you should see the camera's LCD screen light up, and the **Nikon logo** will briefly appear.
   - The viewfinder and the control panel should also be activated, displaying important information such as battery level and shooting settings.

2. Powering Off the Camera

Steps to Turn Off:

1. **Locate the Power Switch**
   - The power switch is still positioned on the **top right** of the camera, next to the mode dial.

2. **Turn the Power Switch Off**
   - Slide the **power switch** back to the **O** (off) position.

3. **Confirm Power-Off**
   - The camera's display should turn off, and the **Nikon logo** will disappear.
   - The camera will stop drawing power, saving the battery for future use.

Important Notes:

- **Auto Power-Off Feature:** The Nikon D7500 has an **auto power-off** feature that automatically turns off the camera after a period of inactivity. This helps conserve battery life when you're not actively using the camera.

- **Battery Management:** Always turn the camera off when not in use, especially if you're not planning to use it for a while. This prevents unnecessary battery drain.

- **Avoid Removing the Battery While On:** Do not remove the battery while the camera is powered on, as it could cause system errors or data corruption, especially when reviewing images or writing to the memory card.

With these simple steps, you can efficiently control the power on your Nikon D7500, extending the lifespan of both the camera and its battery.

CHAPTER THREE

BASIC OPERATIONS

3.1 Understanding the Mode Dial

The Mode Dial on the Nikon D7500 is a key feature for controlling the camera's shooting settings. It allows you to select different modes for automatic or manual control, depending on your skill level and the scene you're capturing. Each mode changes the camera's behavior, including exposure settings like aperture, shutter speed, and ISO.

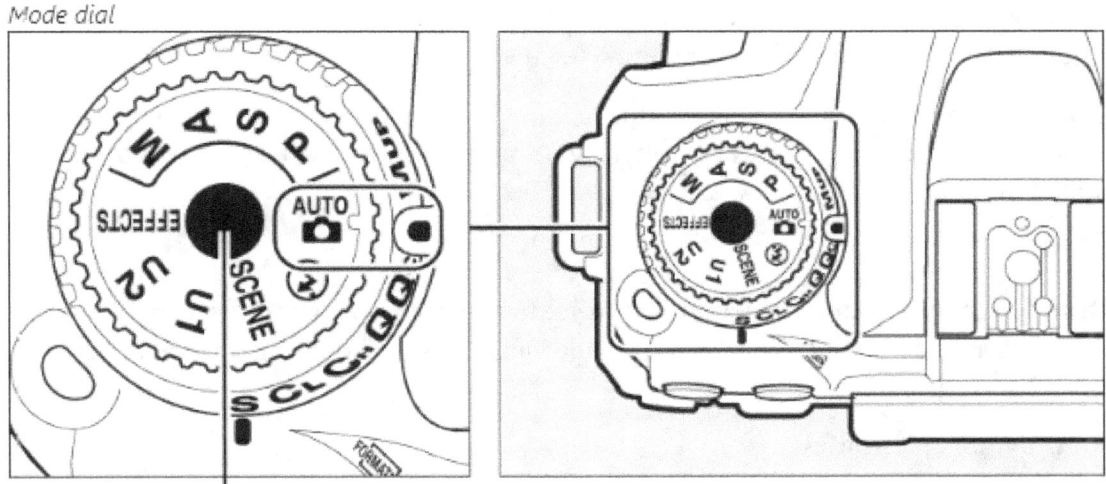

1. The Modes on the Nikon D7500 Mode Dial

The Mode Dial on the Nikon D7500 includes several shooting modes, from fully automatic to full manual control. Below is an overview of each mode and its purpose:

A. Green Auto Mode (Auto)

- **Description:** The camera automatically adjusts all settings (aperture, shutter speed, ISO, etc.) to provide a well-exposed image.
- **Use When:** You want to point and shoot without worrying about settings. Ideal for beginners or when you need quick, effortless shots.

B. Program Auto (P)

- **Description:** The camera automatically sets both aperture and shutter speed, but you have control over ISO and can adjust the exposure compensation.
- **Use When:** You want the camera to select the optimal settings, but still want flexibility to make some adjustments.

C. Shutter Priority (S)

- **Description:** You select the shutter speed, and the camera automatically adjusts the aperture to maintain proper exposure.

- **Use When:** You need to control motion, such as freezing fast-moving subjects or capturing long exposures. Ideal for sports or action shots.

D. Aperture Priority (A)

- **Description:** You select the aperture (f-stop), and the camera automatically adjusts the shutter speed to achieve proper exposure.
- **Use When:** You want to control depth of field, such as for portraits with blurred backgrounds or landscapes with sharp details.

E. Manual Mode (M)

- **Description:** You have full control over both shutter speed and aperture. The camera will not adjust either setting, allowing for complete creative control.
- **Use When:** You want to take full control of exposure settings. Ideal for advanced photographers who want to experiment with creative effects like long exposures or precise lighting control.

F. Scene Modes

- **Description:** The camera selects optimal settings for various types of scenes. These modes are pre-programmed for specific conditions and can be used by rotating the dial to match the scene you're photographing.
- **Common Scene Modes:**
  - **Portrait:** Optimizes settings for portrait photography, blurring the background and highlighting the subject.
  - **Landscape:** Maximizes depth of field to keep both the foreground and background in focus.
  - **Sports:** Sets a fast shutter speed to capture action shots without motion blur.
  - **Night Portrait:** Uses a slower shutter speed and flash to illuminate the subject in low light.

G. Effects Modes

- **Description:** The camera applies various creative effects to your photos. You can choose from options such as **Selective Color, Toy Camera, Miniature, and High Contrast Monochrome**.
- **Use When:** You want to apply artistic effects to your photos directly in-camera.

H. U1 / U2 (User Settings)

- **Description:** These are custom settings that allow you to save and quickly recall your preferred shooting settings. You can customize settings like aperture, shutter speed, ISO, and other options.
- **Use When:** You have a preferred setup for specific situations (e.g., portraits or low light) and want to switch back to that setup easily.

2. Using the Mode Dial

How to Rotate the Mode Dial:

- Simply rotate the dial to select your desired shooting mode.
- If you're unsure which mode to choose, start with **Auto** for quick snapshots or experiment with **Program Auto (P)** for more flexibility.

3. Best Mode for Different Situations

- **Auto Mode** for everyday, casual photography.
- **Shutter Priority (S)** for capturing fast action like sports or moving vehicles.
- **Aperture Priority (A)** for controlling depth of field in portraits or landscapes.
- **Manual Mode (M)** when you want total control over your exposure.
- **Scene Modes** for specific situations like night photography or portrait shots.
- **Effects Modes** for creative, artistic images.

The Mode Dial on the Nikon D7500 allows you to easily switch between automatic and manual settings, giving you the flexibility to shoot in various conditions and achieve the best results. Whether you're a beginner or an advanced photographer, understanding how each mode works will help you maximize the potential of your camera and take better photos.

3.2 Using the Touchscreen

The Nikon D7500 is equipped with a 3.2-inch vari-angle touchscreen LCD, which offers various features that make the camera more intuitive and convenient to use. The touchscreen can be used for a variety of functions, including focusing, capturing photos, and navigating the menu. Here's how to make the most of your camera's touchscreen.

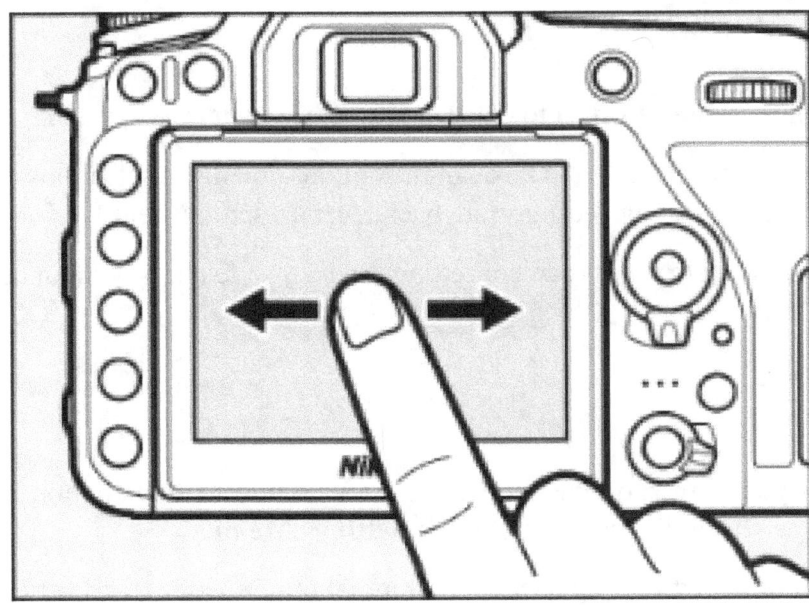

1. Basic Touchscreen Functions

A. Touch to Focus (Tap Focus)

- **How to Use:**
    - In live view mode, simply tap on the area of the LCD screen where you want the camera to focus.
    - The camera will adjust the focus point based on your tap and will automatically adjust the exposure for that area.
- **Use When:** This is ideal for capturing fast-moving subjects or when you're using the camera at odd angles (like when shooting from above or below).

B. Touch Shutter (Touch to Capture)

- **How to Use:**
    - In live view mode, tap the area of the screen where you want to focus, and hold for a moment. The camera will not only focus but also take a photo automatically.
- **Use When:** You need a quick, hands-free way to take a picture, especially in situations where pressing the shutter button might cause camera shake.

C. Swiping to Change Images

- **How to Use:**
    - While reviewing images in playback mode, swipe left or right across the touchscreen to move through your photos.
- **Use When:** You want to quickly scroll through your pictures during review.

2. Navigating the Menu Using the Touchscreen

A. Touch Menu Navigation

- **How to Use:**
    - Tap on the **Menu button** to enter the camera's main menu system.
    - Use the touchscreen to tap through the options and make selections in the various menu categories (shooting settings, playback, custom settings, etc.).
- **Use When:** You want to access camera settings and adjust features without using the directional buttons.

B. Quick Settings Menu

- **How to Use:**
    - When you're in shooting mode, press the **i** (information) button on the back of the camera. This will display the **Quick Settings Menu**.
    - Tap on any setting (e.g., ISO, aperture, shutter speed) to adjust it directly from the touchscreen.

- **Use When:** You need quick access to frequently used settings without diving into the main menu.

3. Using the Vari-Angle Screen

A. Rotating the Screen

- **How to Use:**
    - The Nikon D7500 features a vari-angle touchscreen, meaning you can tilt and rotate the screen to different angles.
    - Rotate the screen outward, upward, or downward depending on your shooting position.
- **Use When:** You want to take photos at high or low angles, or if you need to shoot in live view mode while holding the camera at a non-standard angle (like above your head or close to the ground).

B. Live View Mode

- **How to Use:**
    - Press the **Live View button** to activate the LCD screen as the main viewfinder.
    - You can then use the touchscreen to tap to focus and take pictures as described above.
- **Use When:** You need to use the screen as your viewfinder, particularly when shooting videos or taking photos from unconventional angles.

4. Advanced Touchscreen Features

A. Pinch to Zoom (Playback Mode)

- **How to Use:**
    - In playback mode, pinch your fingers apart on the touchscreen to zoom in on an image.
    - Pinch them together to zoom out.
- **Use When:** You want to closely examine details in your photos during review.

B. Touch Focus and Exposure Control

- **How to Use:**
    - In live view mode, tap to focus, and drag your finger across the screen to adjust the exposure (brightness).
- **Use When:** You want fine control over focus and exposure without adjusting settings manually.

5. Disabling the Touchscreen (Optional)

If you prefer to use the camera without the touchscreen, you can disable it in the camera's settings.

How to Disable:

1. Press the **Menu button** and go to the **Custom Settings Menu**.

2. Navigate to **Controls**.

3. Select **Touch Control** and set it to **Off**.

- **Use When:** You prefer using the physical buttons for all controls, or you find the touchscreen activates unintentionally while holding the camera.

6. Tips for Using the Touchscreen

- **Protection:** The touchscreen is an essential part of your camera, so consider using a screen protector to prevent scratches and damage.

- **Accidental Touches:** Ensure that your hands or fingers don't inadvertently tap the screen while you're composing a shot. The **Lock Touch Function** can help prevent this by disabling the touchscreen during viewfinder use.

- **Cleaning:** Clean the touchscreen regularly with a soft, lint-free cloth to keep it responsive and free of smudges.

The touchscreen on the Nikon D7500 adds a layer of convenience, allowing you to control settings, focus, capture images, and review photos more quickly and intuitively. By mastering the touchscreen's features, you can streamline your photography experience and make the most of your camera's capabilities.

3.3 Navigating the Menu

The Nikon D7500 features an intuitive menu system that allows you to access and adjust various camera settings. Understanding how to navigate this menu efficiently will help you customize your camera to suit your shooting needs and preferences.

1. Accessing the Main Menu

- **Press the Menu Button:**
    - On the back of the camera, press the **Menu** button (located just to the left of the LCD screen).
    - This will display the main menu on the LCD screen, where you can adjust various settings related to shooting, playback, custom settings, and more.

2. Menu Overview

The Nikon D7500 menu is divided into several categories or tabs, each containing related settings. You can scroll through these tabs and options to find the settings you need.

A. Shooting Menu (Camera Icon)

This menu allows you to adjust settings that affect how the camera captures photos and videos.

- **Image Quality and Size:** Adjust JPEG or RAW settings and image resolution.

- **White Balance:** Set the correct colour temperature for various lighting conditions.

- **Auto Focus Mode:** Choose between different autofocus modes (e.g., Single, Continuous, or Auto).

- **Metering Mode:** Select how the camera measures light for exposure (e.g., Matrix, Spot, Centre-weighted).

B. Playback Menu (Playback Icon)

This menu controls settings for viewing and managing your photos and videos.

- **Delete Images:** Delete selected images or all images from the memory card.
- **Slideshow:** Play a slideshow of your captured images.
- **Zoom and Scroll:** Zoom in on images during playback for detailed viewing.

C. Custom Settings Menu (Pencil Icon)

The Custom Settings menu offers more advanced control over how the camera functions.

- **Controls:** Customize button assignments and touchscreen behaviour.
- **Autofocus Settings:** Fine-tune the autofocus system for better performance.
- **Exposure Settings:** Adjust options like bracketing, metering, and more for greater control over exposure.

D. Set Up Menu (Wrench Icon)

This menu controls general camera settings, including those for power, display, and connectivity.

- **Language and Time:** Set your preferred language and adjust the camera's time and date.
- **Image Rotation:** Control how images are rotated in playback.
- **File Naming:** Set custom file names for saved images.

E. Retouch Menu (Paintbrush Icon)

This menu provides options for editing images in-camera, such as applying filters or adjusting exposure.

- **Quick Retouch:** Automatically improve the appearance of an image.
- **Crop:** Crop an image to a specified aspect ratio.
- **Special Effects:** Apply artistic effects like black-and-white or vignette

3. Navigating Through the Menu

A. Using the Directional Buttons

- **Up, Down, Left, Right:** Use the **Multi-selector** (the joystick-like button) to navigate through the menu options. Press up, down, left, or right to move between different settings.
- **Select/OK Button:** Once you highlight the desired setting, press the **OK** button in the center of the Multi-selector to confirm your selection or enter a submenu.

B. Using the Touchscreen (in Live View)

- **Tap to Select:** If you're in **Live View mode**, you can navigate the menu by tapping on the touchscreen to select items and confirm settings.

C. Exiting the Menu

- **Press the Menu Button Again:** To exit the menu, press the **Menu** button once more, or press the **Live View** button to return to shooting mode.

4. Using the Quick Settings Menu

In addition to the main menu, the Nikon D7500 offers a **Quick Settings Menu** that allows you to adjust frequently used settings without diving deep into the full menu system.

- **How to Access:**
    - Press the **i** (information) button on the back of the camera.
    - This will display a customizable set of settings (such as ISO, shutter speed, aperture, etc.).

- **Adjust Settings:**
    - Use the directional buttons or touchscreen to adjust the settings shown in the **Quick Settings Menu**

5. Tips for Efficient Menu Navigation

- **Use Custom Settings:** If you often adjust certain settings, consider customizing the **Quick Settings Menu** or creating **User Presets (U1, U2)** on the Mode Dial to save time.

- **Practice Navigation:** Spend some time getting familiar with the layout of the menus. Once you're comfortable, navigating between settings will be faster and more intuitive.

- **Menu Shortcuts:** Many settings can be accessed directly from the **Info Display** (press **i**) or the **Live View** screen, which can save time when adjusting common settings like ISO, white balance, or focus mode.

The menu system on the Nikon D7500 offers a wide range of options to customize your camera's behavior and optimize your shooting experience. By learning how to navigate the menu efficiently, you'll be able to adjust settings on the fly, ensuring you get the best results from your camera in any situation.

3.4 Setting the Date, Time, and Language

Properly setting the date, time, and language on your Nikon D7500 ensures that your photos and videos are correctly timestamped, and that you can navigate the camera's menus in your preferred language. Here's how to configure these settings:

1. Setting the Date and Time

A. Steps to Set the Date and Time:

1. **Turn On the Camera:**
   - Press the **Power button** to turn on your Nikon D7500.

2. **Access the Menu:**
   - Press the **Menu button** on the back of the camera.

3. **Navigate to the Setup Menu:**
   - Using the **Multi-selector** (the directional buttons or touchscreen), scroll to the **Set Up Menu** (indicated by the wrench icon).

4. **Select Date and Time:**
   - In the **Set Up Menu**, scroll down and select **Time Zone and Date**.
   - This will display the **Date and Time settings** screen.

5. **Set the Time Zone:**
   - Use the **Multi-selector** to choose your time zone.
   - Tap or press **OK** once your time zone is selected.

6. **Adjust the Date and Time:**
   - Next, you'll be prompted to enter the **Date** (month, day, year) and **Time** (hour, minute).
   - Use the **Multi-selector** to highlight the value you want to change (e.g., month, day, hour).
   - Press the **OK** button to confirm each value, and use the **Multi-selector** to adjust the numbers.

7. **Finish and Confirm:**
   - Once you've set the correct date and time, press **OK** to confirm your settings.
   - The camera will now use the updated date and time for all future images.

2. Setting the Language

A. Steps to Set the Language:

1. **Turn On the Camera:**
   - Press the **Power button** to turn on your Nikon D7500.

2. **Access the Menu:**
    - Press the **Menu button** to open the camera's main menu.

3. **Navigate to the Setup Menu:**
    - Scroll to the **Set Up Menu** (wrench icon) using the **Multi-selector**.

4. **Select Language:**
    - In the **Set Up Menu**, scroll down to select **Language**.
    - Tap **OK** to enter the language selection screen.

5. **Choose Your Preferred Language:**
    - Scroll through the list of available languages.
    - Use the **Multi-selector** to select your preferred language and press **OK** to confirm.

6. **Finish:**
    - The menu will now display in the language you've selected.

3. Tips and Considerations

- **Time Zone Settings:** If you travel frequently across time zones, the Nikon D7500 allows you to adjust the time zone without having to manually reset the time each time. Just update it in the **Time Zone and Date** settings.

- **Date Format:** The camera uses the format **MM/DD/YYYY** by default, but you can adjust it if you are in a region where a different format is preferred.

- **Battery Backup:** The camera will retain your date, time, and language settings even when turned off, thanks to an internal battery.

Setting the correct date, time, and language on your Nikon D7500 is essential for accurate photo metadata and a user-friendly experience. By following the steps above, you can ensure that your camera is properly configured for your shooting needs and preferences.

CHAPTER FOUR
SHOOTING BASICS

4.1 Auto Mode: Point-and-Shoot Simplicity

The Auto Mode on the Nikon D7500 is designed to provide you with a simple, hassle-free shooting experience, allowing you to capture high-quality images without worrying about adjusting manual settings. It's perfect for beginners or when you want to focus entirely on composition without getting into technical details. Here's how to use Auto Mode and make the most of it.

1. Understanding Auto Mode

Auto Mode is a fully automated shooting mode where the camera handles all the important settings like exposure, shutter speed, aperture, ISO, and white balance. The camera automatically adjusts these settings based on the scene it detects, allowing you to focus solely on framing your shot.

- **Icon:** The Auto Mode is represented by a green **camera icon** on the **Mode Dial**.

- **Purpose:** Ideal for capturing quick snapshots with minimal effort, this mode is great for everyday photography, casual moments, and when you want the camera to make decisions for you.

2. How to Use Auto Mode

A. Setting the Camera to Auto Mode

1. **Turn on the Camera:**
   - Press the **Power button** to power on the Nikon D7500.

2. **Select Auto Mode:**
   - Turn the **Mode Dial** (located on the top of the camera) to the **Auto** setting, marked with a green camera icon.

3. **Ready to Shoot:**
   - The camera will automatically set the correct exposure, white balance, and ISO based on the scene you're capturing.
   - Simply compose your shot through the **viewfinder** or **LCD screen** (if you're using Live View).

B. Taking the Shot

- **Press the Shutter Button:**
   - Half-press the **shutter button** to focus on your subject, and fully press it to capture the image.
   - The camera will handle all the exposure settings, adjusting them as needed for proper exposure.

3. Benefits of Using Auto Mode

A. Simplicity and Convenience

- **Point-and-Shoot:** Auto Mode allows you to instantly capture photos with minimal setup and understanding of camera settings.
- **No Worry About Settings:** You don't need to adjust ISO, shutter speed, or aperture — the camera takes care of it all for you.

B. Reliable Results

- **Optimized Settings:** The camera automatically selects the best exposure settings based on lighting conditions, subject matter, and focus.
- **Consistent Performance:** In most scenarios, Auto Mode will deliver well-balanced and properly exposed images.

C. Ideal for Beginners

- **Learning Tool:** Auto Mode is a great way for new users to learn the basics of photography without getting overwhelmed by manual settings.
- **Stress-Free Photography:** Whether you're capturing a family gathering, vacation moments, or street photography, Auto Mode allows you to focus on composition and creativity rather than technical aspects.

4. When to Use Auto Mode

- **Casual Moments:** When you need to take photos quickly without worrying about settings, such as at social events or travel situations.
- **Unpredictable Scenes:** When you're unsure about the best settings for a scene, Auto Mode is a great option since it automatically adjusts to lighting and subject conditions.
- **Low-Light Conditions:** The camera automatically adjusts the ISO and shutter speed to help achieve the best results in low-light environments.

5. Limitations of Auto Mode

While Auto Mode is very convenient, it does have a few limitations:

A. Limited Creative Control

- **No Manual Adjustments:** You can't directly control settings like aperture or shutter speed, which can limit your ability to achieve creative effects (e.g., shallow depth of field or motion blur).
- **Lack of Customization:** For photographers who want to push their creative boundaries, Auto Mode might not provide the flexibility needed for more advanced techniques.

B. Scene Limitations

- **Basic Scene Recognition:** Auto Mode works well in typical situations but may struggle with complex lighting or highly detailed compositions. It might not always adjust settings to the ideal exposure in challenging environments.

6. Enhancing Your Shots in Auto Mode

Although Auto Mode handles the technical side of things, there are a few simple tips to enhance your images:

A. Use the Touchscreen (Live View)

- In **Live View** mode, you can use the **touchscreen** to tap on your subject for focusing, which may help you get a sharper focus, especially when photographing objects or people.

B. Composition Techniques

- Even in Auto Mode, composition plays a big role in creating visually appealing photographs. Follow basic rules like the **Rule of Thirds**, framing, and leading lines for better results.

C. Take Advantage of Scene Modes (Optional)

- If you want a bit more control, the Nikon D7500 offers specific **Scene Modes** (like Portrait, Landscape, Night Portrait, etc.) that are pre-configured for different scenarios. These modes are accessible from the Mode Dial and provide more tailored settings for particular types of shots.

7. Switching Out of Auto Mode

As you gain experience, you may want to experiment with other modes that give you more control over your photos, such as:

- **Programmed Auto (P Mode):** The camera still controls most settings, but you can adjust the ISO and other options.

- **Aperture Priority (A Mode):** You control the aperture, while the camera automatically adjusts shutter speed.

- **Shutter Priority (S Mode):** You control shutter speed, and the camera adjusts aperture.

Auto Mode on the Nikon D7500 offers a simple, reliable, and quick way to capture images without needing to worry about manual settings. Whether you're a beginner or need a straightforward point-and-shoot option, Auto Mode allows you to get the shot while the camera handles the technical details. Once you're comfortable, you can gradually explore more advanced modes to take full advantage of the camera's capabilities.

4.2 Using Live View

The Live View feature on the Nikon D7500 allows you to capture photos and videos using the LCD screen instead of the viewfinder. It's especially useful for composing shots at unusual angles, shooting video, and taking still images in situations where you want a wider view of the scene. Here's how to effectively use Live View and make the most of this feature.

1. Activating Live View

A. Steps to Activate Live View:

1. **Turn On the Camera:**

   o Press the **Power button** to turn on your Nikon D7500.

2. **Switch to Live View Mode:**

   o Press the **LV (Live View) button** located to the right of the viewfinder. This will activate the Live View mode, and you'll see the image on the **LCD screen**.

3. **Composition via LCD:**

   o With Live View enabled, you can now compose your shot using the **LCD screen** rather than the viewfinder.

B. Live View Modes

- **Shooting Mode:** Live View can be used in most shooting modes (Auto, Program, Aperture Priority, etc.). It provides a real-time preview of your composition, allowing you to see how the image will look before capturing it.

- **Video Recording Mode:** You can also switch to **Movie mode** in Live View to record high-quality video. The camera will display a live feed of your scene, and you can adjust settings before recording.

2. Using Live View for Photography

A. Focus Mode

Live View allows you to choose between two focusing modes:

1. **Contrast-Auto Focus (AF):**

   o This is the default autofocus mode in Live View. The camera will adjust the focus by comparing contrast levels in the image and adjusting the lens accordingly.

   o **How to Use:**

   - Half-press the **shutter button** to initiate autofocus.

   - The camera will automatically focus on the area of highest contrast within the frame.

   - You'll see the focus point highlighted on the screen as it adjusts.

2. **Manual Focus (MF):**
    - If you want more control over focus, you can switch to manual focus mode and adjust the lens yourself.
    - **How to Use:**
        - Switch the lens to the **MF** position and manually turn the focus ring.
        - The screen will often show a magnified view of the area you are focusing on, helping you achieve precise focus.

B. Exposure Preview

One of the main advantages of Live View is that it allows you to preview how the image will appear with your current settings.

- **Real-time Exposure Adjustments:** As you adjust the aperture, shutter speed, or ISO, the image displayed on the LCD screen will adjust in real-time, giving you a clear view of exposure and depth of field.
- **Exposure Simulation:** This feature helps you make quick adjustments to ensure the image is neither too bright nor too dark before capturing the shot.

C. Composition Assistance

- **Grid Lines:** To help with composition, you can enable grid lines for alignment. This is useful for framing your subject according to the **Rule of Thirds** or ensuring straight horizons in landscape shots.
- **Focus Peaking (if enabled):** For manual focusing, some cameras feature focus peaking, which highlights in-focus areas in the frame to help you achieve sharp focus.

3. Using Live View for Video Recording

A. Switching to Video Mode

1. **Activate Movie Mode:**
    - Turn the Mode Dial to **Movie Mode** (the **red camera icon**).
    - Alternatively, while in Live View, press the **Record button** to start video recording directly from Live View mode.
2. **Start Recording:**
    - Press the **Record button** (the red dot) on the back of the camera to begin recording.
    - The LCD screen will show the live video feed, and the camera will continue recording until you press the **Record button** again to stop.
3. **Manual Controls (Optional):**
    - You can adjust settings like aperture, ISO, and shutter speed manually to control the exposure while recording.

- o **Autofocus:** In video mode, you can choose to use **Continuous Autofocus (AF-C)** for smooth focus transitions during recording.

4. Benefits of Using Live View

A. Flexible Composition

- **Shooting from Angles:** Live View allows you to shoot from high or low angles without needing to look through the viewfinder. This makes it easier to frame shots, especially for creative photography like macro shots or selfies.

- **More Control Over Focus:** In manual focus mode, Live View gives you a magnified view of the scene, which helps you focus precisely, especially for detailed subjects.

B. Easy Composition in Difficult Lighting

- **Preview Exposure and Depth of Field:** With Live View, you can see how your settings affect the final image in real-time, which is especially helpful in low light or difficult lighting conditions.

C. Video Recording Convenience

- **Continuous Viewing:** Live View is the primary mode for video recording on the D7500, offering a continuous live preview for composition and monitoring.

- **Autofocus While Recording:** The camera can autofocus during video recording, allowing you to capture smooth video footage without manual focus adjustments.

5. Limitations of Live View

A. Autofocus Speed

- In Live View, autofocus is generally slower than using the viewfinder, especially in **Contrast-AF** mode. This is because the camera has to analyze the image in real-time to adjust the focus, which can result in slower focusing speeds compared to the traditional **Phase Detection AF** used with the viewfinder.

B. Battery Consumption

- Using Live View drains the battery more quickly since the LCD screen is constantly active. It's a good idea to carry extra batteries if you plan to shoot for extended periods with Live View enabled.

6. Tips for Using Live View

- **Use the LCD Screen for Precise Framing:** When using Live View, take advantage of the large LCD screen for better composition and more precise framing.

- **Activate the Histogram:** To monitor exposure levels, enable the histogram display in Live View mode. This can help you avoid overexposure or underexposure in your shots.

- **Utilize Focus Magnification:** For fine-tuning focus in manual mode, magnify a section of the image by pressing the **magnify button** on the back of the camera. This will zoom in on your subject, making it easier to achieve sharp focus.

Live View on the Nikon D7500 offers an intuitive way to compose your shots and videos, especially in situations where the viewfinder is hard to use, or you need a more detailed preview of the scene. Whether you're capturing stills at unique angles or recording high-quality video, Live View enhances your flexibility and creative control. While it may have some limitations, particularly in autofocus speed and battery consumption, it remains a valuable feature for modern photography and videography.

4.3 Adjusting Focus Modes (AF-S, AF-C, Manual Focus)

The focus mode on your Nikon D7500 is essential for ensuring your subject is captured with the sharpest focus possible. You have several focus modes to choose from, each designed for different types of subjects and shooting scenarios. Understanding when and how to use AF-S (Single-servo autofocus), AF-C (Continuous-servo autofocus), and Manual Focus (MF) will help you take control of your focus settings for optimal results.

1. Understanding Focus Modes

- **AF-S (Single-servo Autofocus):** This mode is designed for stationary subjects. The camera focuses once when you half-press the shutter button and locks the focus. Once the subject is in focus, the camera will maintain that focus as long as you don't release the shutter button.

- **AF-C (Continuous-servo Autofocus):** This mode is ideal for moving subjects. The camera continuously adjusts the focus as long as you half-press the shutter button. This is especially useful for action shots, sports photography, or wildlife where the subject is constantly changing distance.

- **Manual Focus (MF):** In this mode, you have full control over the focus by adjusting the lens's focus ring yourself. This is helpful when autofocus isn't reliable, such as in low light, when photographing still subjects like macro photography, or when you want to focus precisely on a specific point.

2. How to Adjust Focus Modes

A. Using the Focus Mode Switch on the Camera

1. **Locate the Focus Mode Switch:**
   - On the Nikon D7500, the **focus mode switch** is located on the front of the camera, near the lens mount.
   - It has three settings: **AF-S**, **AF-C**, and **MF**.

2. **Change Focus Mode:**
   - Slide the switch to **AF-S** for Single-servo autofocus (best for stationary subjects).
   - Slide the switch to **AF-C** for Continuous-servo autofocus (best for moving subjects).
   - Slide the switch to **MF** for Manual Focus (best for manual adjustments).

B. Adjusting Focus Modes via the Camera Menu (if needed)

1. **Turn on the Camera:**
   - Press the **Power button** to turn on your Nikon D7500.

2. **Open the Menu:**
    - Press the **Menu button** to bring up the camera's menu.
3. **Navigate to the Focus Settings:**
    - Scroll through the menu using the **Multi-selector** and go to the **Custom Settings Menu (Pencil icon)**.
    - Select **Autofocus** (AF) to access advanced autofocus settings.
4. **Choose Focus Mode:**
    - You can change the focus mode (AF-S, AF-C, or MF) from this menu as well, depending on the scenario.

3. When to Use Each Focus Mode

A. AF-S (Single-servo Autofocus)

- **When to Use:**
    - When photographing stationary or slow-moving subjects.
    - Ideal for portraits, landscapes, or still-life photography.
    - Works best in **good lighting** conditions when the subject isn't moving.
- **How it Works:**
    - When you half-press the shutter button, the camera locks the focus on the subject.
    - Once the subject is in focus, the camera will hold the focus, and you can fully press the shutter to take the shot.
- **Tips:**
    - Use **AF-S** if your subject is stationary and you want to ensure precise focus before capturing the image.

B. AF-C (Continuous-servo Autofocus)

- **When to Use:**
    - When photographing moving subjects, such as in sports, wildlife, or action shots.
    - Ideal for tracking subjects that are constantly changing position or distance from the camera.
- **How it Works:**
    - The camera continuously adjusts the focus as long as you half-press the shutter button. This allows the camera to track the subject's movement and keep it in focus even as it changes position.
    - It's especially helpful for moving subjects that you can't predict.

- **Tips:**
  - Use **AF-C** when photographing moving subjects like runners, cars, or birds in flight. It will ensure the camera adjusts focus to keep your subject sharp as it moves.

C. MF (Manual Focus)

- **When to Use:**
  - In situations where autofocus is unreliable, such as in low light, macro photography, or when shooting through obstacles like glass or fences.
  - Ideal when you want **precise control** over the focus point, such as in still-life or landscape photography.

- **How it Works:**
  - You manually turn the focus ring on the lens to adjust focus. This is useful when autofocus struggles with subjects like low-contrast scenes or objects in motion.
  - On the Nikon D7500, you can enable **focus magnification** in the Live View mode to assist you in manually focusing with greater precision.

- **Tips:**
  - **Focus magnification** (press the + button during Live View) can help you manually adjust focus with more precision. This is especially helpful in macro or portrait photography, where fine focus adjustments are needed.

4. Additional Focus Options and Settings

A. Focus Area Settings

- The Nikon D7500 allows you to choose different **focus area modes** for AF-S and AF-C. This determines how the camera selects the area to focus on. Options include:
  - **Single-point AF:** Choose a specific point in the frame for precise focusing.
  - **Dynamic-area AF:** The camera uses several points to track a moving subject.
  - **3D-tracking:** The camera automatically tracks and adjusts focus on a subject based on its movement.

B. Focus Lock

- If you're using **AF-S** but want to focus on a subject and reframe your shot, you can lock focus by holding down the **AE-L/AF-L button**. This will lock focus even if you release the shutter button.

C. Focus Assist

- In situations where you're in **MF** mode, you can use **focus assist** to magnify a portion of the image on the LCD screen, making it easier to fine-tune your manual focus.

Choosing the right focus mode—**AF-S, AF-C,** or **MF**—is essential for capturing sharp, well-focused images. By understanding the purpose of each focus mode, you can tailor your approach to various shooting conditions, ensuring that your subjects are always in perfect focus, whether they're still or in motion. Whether you're capturing a portrait, shooting a fast-moving athlete, or manually focusing on a small object, mastering the different focus modes of your Nikon D7500 will help you take full control of your photography.

4.4 Exposure Modes (P, S, A, M)

The Nikon D7500 offers four primary exposure modes—P (Program), S (Shutter Priority), A (Aperture Priority), and M (Manual)—each designed for different levels of control over the exposure settings. Understanding these modes will help you achieve the right exposure in various shooting conditions. Here's a breakdown of each mode:

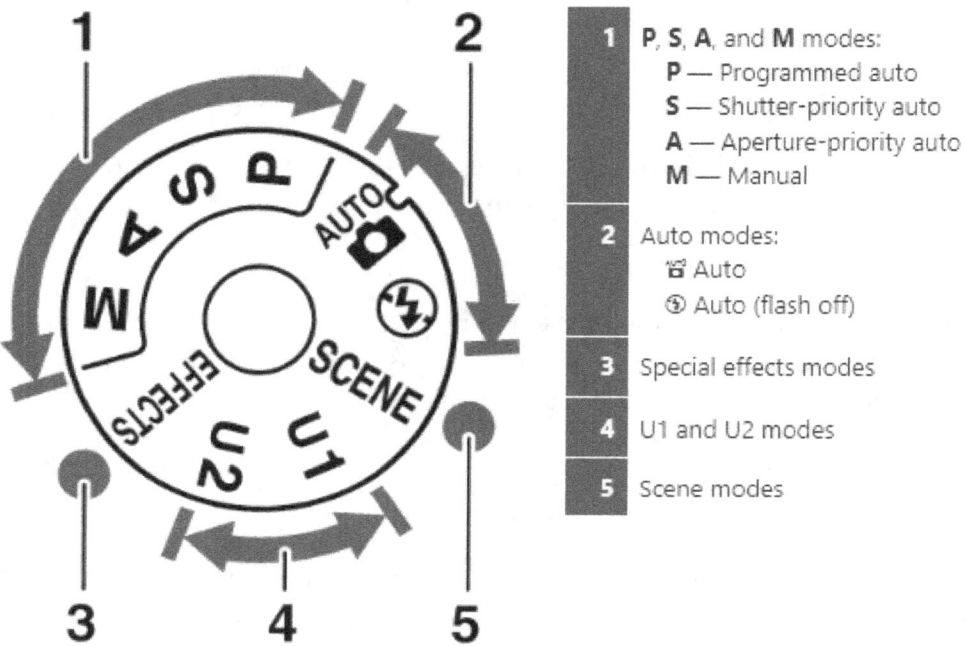

1. P - Program Mode

Program Mode (P) is a fully automated shooting mode that provides some flexibility while still allowing the camera to decide on key exposure settings.

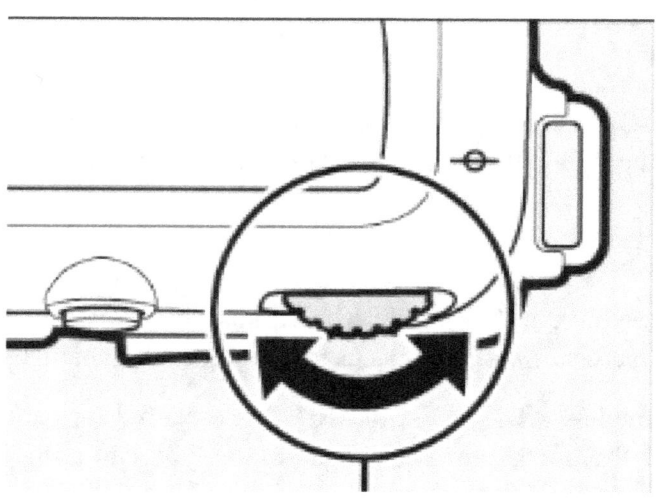

How it Works:

- In **P Mode**, the camera automatically selects both the **shutter speed** and **aperture** to give you a well-exposed image based on the lighting conditions.
- You can adjust **ISO** manually, but the camera will control the aperture and shutter speed for proper exposure.

Flexibility:

- **Flexible Program:** In **P Mode**, you can adjust the exposure settings by rotating the **main command dial**. This allows you to change the combination of shutter speed and aperture while keeping the same exposure value. This feature is known as **Flexible Program**.

When to Use:

- Ideal for **general shooting** when you want convenience but still have the ability to adjust certain settings (like ISO).
- Good for subjects that aren't moving quickly and when you don't want to spend much time adjusting settings.

2. S - Shutter Priority Mode

Shutter Priority Mode (S) gives you control over the **shutter speed**, while the camera automatically adjusts the aperture for a proper exposure.

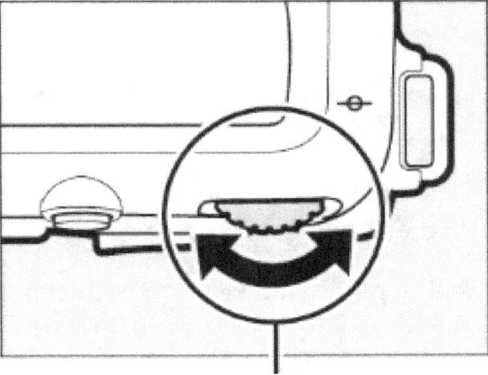

Main command dial

How it Works:

- In **S Mode**, you set the **shutter speed**, and the camera automatically selects the appropriate **aperture** based on the scene's lighting conditions.
- **Shutter Speed Control:** This is ideal for controlling motion. A fast shutter speed (e.g., 1/500s) will freeze fast-moving subjects, while a slower shutter speed (e.g., 1/30s) will create motion blur.

When to Use:

- **Fast-moving subjects:** Ideal for **sports, wildlife**, or any situation where you need to control motion. A fast shutter speed helps freeze action, while a slow shutter speed can create a sense of movement.

- **Low light situations:** In low-light conditions, you might want to use a slower shutter speed to let in more light, but be mindful of camera shake (using a tripod or higher ISO can help).

3. A - Aperture Priority Mode

Aperture Priority Mode (A) gives you control over the **aperture** (f-stop), while the camera automatically adjusts the **shutter speed** to maintain proper exposure.

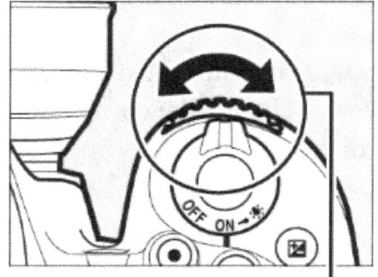

Sub-command dial

How it Works:

- In **A Mode**, you control the aperture to adjust the **depth of field**, and the camera will select the appropriate **shutter speed** based on the lighting conditions.
- **Aperture Control:** A **wide aperture** (e.g., f/2.8) will create a shallow depth of field, blurring the background and isolating the subject. A **small aperture** (e.g., f/16) will keep more of the scene in focus, which is useful for landscapes.

When to Use:

- **Portraits:** When you want to blur the background and make the subject stand out, a wide aperture (low f-number) is ideal.
- **Landscapes:** When you want a larger depth of field to keep the foreground and background in focus, a smaller aperture (higher f-number) is preferred.
- **Low light:** In low-light conditions, a wide aperture will let more light in, which helps achieve a proper exposure.

4. M - Manual Mode

Manual Mode (M) provides full control over both the **shutter speed** and **aperture**, allowing you to determine exactly how your image will be exposed.

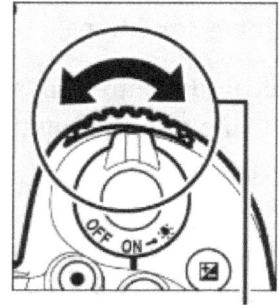

Sub-command dial

How it Works:

- In **M Mode**, you adjust both the **shutter speed** and **aperture** manually.
- The camera will display a **metering scale** in the viewfinder or on the LCD screen to indicate whether the exposure is too dark (underexposed) or too bright (overexposed). You can adjust the settings until the meter indicates a balanced exposure.

When to Use:

- **Creative Control:** When you want complete control over your exposure, such as in **landscape photography**, **long exposure photography**, or **studio setups**.
- **Challenging Lighting Conditions:** When shooting in tricky lighting or when you want to make creative choices with exposure, such as controlling motion with long shutter speeds or achieving a specific **depth of field** for artistic effect.

Comparison of the Exposure Modes (P, S, A, M)

Mode	You Control	Camera Controls	Best for
P	ISO	Shutter speed & Aperture	General shooting with convenience
S	Shutter Speed	Aperture	Moving subjects, sports, wildlife
A	Aperture	Shutter Speed	Portraits, landscapes, low light
M	Shutter Speed & Aperture	None (Full manual control)	Creative control, challenging lighting

Tips for Each Exposure Mode

P Mode Tips:

- Use **P Mode** when you need quick, automatic exposure with some flexibility.
- It's ideal for general photography when you don't want to worry about adjusting both shutter speed and aperture but still want to tweak settings like ISO.

S Mode Tips:

- Use **S Mode** for action shots where the motion speed is important. For fast-moving subjects like athletes or wildlife, use a fast shutter speed (1/500s or higher).
- For creating motion blur in things like flowing water or light trails, use a slower shutter speed.

A Mode Tips:

- In **A Mode**, choose a **wide aperture** for **portraits** to blur the background and isolate the subject. A narrow aperture is great for landscapes when you want maximum depth of field.
- When shooting in low light, open the aperture as wide as possible to gather more light.

M Mode Tips:

- **M Mode** offers total creative freedom, but it requires more attention to detail. Use it when shooting in tricky light conditions, such as backlighting, or when you need to use long exposure times (e.g., capturing night scenes).

- Be mindful of the metering scale in the viewfinder or LCD screen to make sure the exposure is balanced.

Each of the exposure modes—P, S, A, and M—offers varying degrees of control over your camera's settings. While P Mode is perfect for quick, automatic shooting, S, A, and M modes give you more creative control for more specific needs, such as capturing motion, controlling depth of field, or adjusting exposure for artistic purposes. By mastering these modes, you can elevate your photography and adapt to any shooting situation.

4.5 Using Scene and Effect Modes

The Nikon D7500 provides a variety of Scene Modes and Effect Modes that can help you quickly capture high-quality images in different environments without needing to adjust settings manually. These modes are designed for specific types of scenes or creative effects and allow you to focus on your subject while the camera adjusts the exposure, shutter speed, and other settings.

1. Scene Modes

Scene Modes are preset configurations that optimize the camera's settings for specific shooting conditions or types of subjects. These modes are perfect for those who want great results with minimal effort. Below are the available Scene Modes on the Nikon D7500:

A. Portrait Mode

- **Purpose:** Designed for photographing people, this mode optimizes settings for a shallow depth of field to blur the background and make the subject stand out.

- **Best for:** Portrait photography, close-up shots of individuals, and headshots.

B. Landscape Mode

- **Purpose:** This mode adjusts the camera's settings for sharp, clear shots with deep depth of field, ensuring that both the foreground and background are in focus.

- **Best for:** Landscapes, wide outdoor scenes, and architectural photography.

C. Close-up Mode (Macro)

- **Purpose:** The camera sets up for close-up photography with sharp details of small subjects like flowers, insects, or objects with intricate textures.

- **Best for:** Macro photography, capturing fine details in nature, or still-life objects.

D. Sports Mode

- **Purpose:** Optimized for fast-moving subjects, this mode uses a fast shutter speed to freeze action and reduce motion blur.

- **Best for:** Sports, wildlife, or any action shots where you want to capture movement clearly.

E. Night Portrait Mode

- **Purpose:** This mode is designed for capturing well-lit portraits in low light. It uses a slower shutter speed to allow ambient light into the photo while firing the flash to illuminate the subject.
- **Best for:** Portraits taken at night or in low-light environments, with a balanced exposure for both the subject and background.

F. Party/Indoor Mode

- **Purpose:** This mode is perfect for indoor photography in low-light conditions. The camera uses a slower shutter speed and higher ISO to brighten the scene while adjusting flash settings for balanced lighting.
- **Best for:** Indoor events, parties, or dimly lit environments.

G. Beach/Snow Mode

- **Purpose:** This mode helps prevent underexposure of subjects in bright, reflective environments like snow or sand. The camera adjusts the settings to ensure that bright areas aren't overexposed while maintaining detail in the scene.
- **Best for:** Beach photography, snow scenes, or any bright, reflective surface.

H. Sunset Mode

- **Purpose:** Optimized for capturing the warm colours and tones during sunset. This mode adjusts the settings to preserve rich colours and detail in both the sky and landscape.
- **Best for:** Sunset photography, capturing the vibrant colours during dusk or dawn.

I. Dawn/Dusk Mode

- **Purpose:** This mode is tailored for capturing soft light during the early morning or evening hours. It balances the exposure to capture both bright and dark areas in low-light conditions.
- **Best for:** Early morning or evening photography when the lighting is soft and diffused.

2. Effect Modes

Effect Modes add creative filters and effects to your photos to give them a unique look or style. The camera applies the effect in real time, so you can see how the image will look before you take the shot.

A. Selective Colour

- **Purpose:** The camera captures the scene in black and white, while retaining one colour (or a few selected colours) in the image, creating a striking contrast.
- **Best for:** Creative photography when you want to emphasize a single colour in the scene, such as a red flower in a black-and-white background.

B. Miniature Effect

- **Purpose:** This effect creates a "miniature" look by blurring the top and bottom of the image, simulating a tilt-shift effect.
- **Best for:** Creating the illusion of photographing a miniature scene, such as a cityscape or crowded place.

C. Toy Camera Effect

- **Purpose:** This effect gives your photos a vintage, toy-camera look by adding a vignette around the edges and adjusting the colour balance for a retro feel.
- **Best for:** Adding a nostalgic or whimsical touch to your photos, ideal for portraits or artistic shots.

D. High Dynamic Range (HDR)

- **Purpose:** This mode combines multiple exposures of the same scene to create an image with a wider range of light and shadow details. It's perfect for scenes with high contrast, such as bright skies and dark foregrounds.
- **Best for:** Landscape photography or high-contrast scenes where you want to capture both bright and dark details.

E. Soft Focus

- **Purpose:** The camera creates a soft focus effect that blurs the edges of the photo, giving it a dreamy or ethereal quality. This is often used to emphasize the subject and create a romantic or artistic feel.
- **Best for:** Portraits, still life, or artistic photography where you want a gentle, soft look.

F. Watercolour Effect

- **Purpose:** This effect turns your photo into a watercolour painting, enhancing colours and adding a brushstroke-like texture.
- **Best for:** Artistic or abstract photography where you want to create a painterly look.

G. Colour Sketch

- **Purpose:** This mode turns your photo into a colourful sketch with visible lines and soft colours, mimicking the appearance of a hand-drawn pencil or coloured sketch.
- **Best for:** Creative portraits, still life, or artistic photos that you want to look like a sketch or painting.

H. Silhouette

- **Purpose:** The camera captures a strong backlit subject, adjusting the exposure so the subject appears as a dark silhouette against a bright background.
- **Best for:** Creative portraiture where you want to emphasize shape or form rather than detail, such as a person against a sunset or bright sky.

How to Use Scene and Effect Modes

A. Switching to Scene Mode:

1. Turn the mode dial to the **Scene** icon on the Nikon D7500.
2. Use the **multi-selector** or the **touchscreen** to choose the desired Scene Mode (e.g., Portrait, Landscape, Sports).
3. Press the **shutter button** to take your photo.

B. Switching to Effect Mode:

1. Turn the mode dial to **Effects**.
2. Choose the effect you want to apply from the options available.
3. The camera will preview the effect in the LCD screen. When satisfied, press the **shutter button** to capture the image.

When to Use Scene and Effect Modes

- **Scene Modes:** Perfect for quick, automatic settings in a variety of shooting conditions. Great for beginners or anyone who wants good results without adjusting complex settings.
- **Effect Modes:** Ideal for creative and artistic shots when you want to add a unique, stylized look to your images without needing to edit them afterward.

The Scene Modes on the Nikon D7500 provide automatic settings that are optimized for a wide range of situations, from portrait photography to sports and landscapes. Meanwhile, the Effect Modes give you creative control over how your images appear, allowing you to apply filters and effects to achieve unique and artistic looks. Whether you're a beginner or an advanced photographer, these modes help you capture great images in less time while also offering room for creative expression.

CHAPTER FIVE
ADVANCED SHOOTING TECHNIQUES

5.1 Understanding ISO, Shutter Speed, and Aperture

When it comes to photography, three fundamental settings—ISO, shutter speed, and aperture—determine the exposure of your image. These three elements work together to control the amount of light that reaches the camera sensor and influence the final image's brightness, clarity, and creative effects like motion blur or depth of field.

1. ISO: Sensitivity to Light

ISO refers to the **sensitivity** of the camera's sensor to light. The higher the ISO number, the more sensitive the sensor is, meaning it can capture images in lower light conditions without using a flash. However, higher ISO values can also introduce **digital noise**, which appears as graininess in your photos.

How ISO Affects Exposure:

- **Low ISO (e.g., 100 or 200):** Best for bright lighting conditions. It results in clear, crisp images with little to no noise.

- **High ISO (e.g., 1600, 3200, or higher):** Useful in low-light environments, allowing you to capture images without using a flash. However, higher ISO can increase noise and reduce image quality.

When to Adjust ISO:

- **Bright light conditions (outdoors during the day):** Use low ISO (e.g., 100–400) for optimal image quality.

- **Low light conditions (indoors or night):** Increase ISO to 800, 1600, or higher depending on the available light, but be mindful of the noise levels.

ISO Tips:

- **Use Auto ISO:** The Nikon D7500 has an Auto ISO feature that adjusts the ISO automatically based on the lighting conditions. You can set a maximum ISO limit to prevent too much noise.

- **Balancing ISO with Shutter Speed and Aperture:** In low light, increasing ISO may allow you to use faster shutter speeds or smaller apertures to get a well-exposed image.

2. Shutter Speed: Controlling Motion

Shutter speed (or **exposure time**) refers to how long the camera's shutter stays open to let light hit the sensor. It is measured in seconds or fractions of a second (e.g., 1/1000s, 1/500s, 1/30s, 1s). A fast shutter speed captures motion sharply, while a slow shutter speed allows movement to be captured with a blur.

How Shutter Speed Affects Exposure:

- **Fast Shutter Speed (e.g., 1/1000s, 1/500s):** Freezes fast-moving subjects, resulting in a sharp image.

- **Slow Shutter Speed (e.g., 1/30s, 1s):** Captures motion blur, useful for creating effects like flowing water or light trails.

When to Adjust Shutter Speed:

- **Fast-moving subjects (e.g., sports, wildlife):** Use faster shutter speeds to freeze the motion and avoid blur. Start with 1/500s or faster, depending on the speed of the subject.
- **Low-light or artistic effects:** For night photography or long exposure shots, slower shutter speeds (e.g., 1s or longer) can be used to capture more light or create motion effects, such as light trails or blurred movement.

Shutter Speed Tips:

- **Avoid Camera Shake:** If your shutter speed is too slow (e.g., below 1/60s), you risk introducing **camera shake** unless you use a tripod or stabilize the camera. As a general rule, use a shutter speed equal to or faster than the **focal length** of your lens (e.g., for a 50mm lens, use at least 1/50s).
- **Motion Blur for Effect:** Slower shutter speeds can intentionally blur moving subjects, like water flowing or car headlights at night, for artistic effects

3. Aperture: Controlling Depth of Field

Aperture is the size of the opening in the lens that controls the amount of light entering the camera. It's measured in **f-stop** values (e.g., f/1.8, f/4, f/16). A lower f-number means a **wider aperture**, allowing more light into the camera and creating a **shallow depth of field**. A higher f-number means a **narrower aperture**, letting in less light and increasing the **depth of field** (the area in focus).

How Aperture Affects Exposure:

- **Wide Aperture (low f-number like f/1.8 or f/2.8):** Lets in more light and creates a shallow depth of field, which isolates the subject from the background (useful for portraits).
- **Narrow Aperture (high f-number like f/16 or f/22):** Lets in less light and increases the depth of field, keeping more of the scene in focus (useful for landscapes).

When to Adjust Aperture:

- **Portrait Photography:** Use a wide aperture (e.g., f/1.8 or f/2.8) to blur the background and make the subject stand out.
- **Landscape Photography:** Use a narrow aperture (e.g., f/8 to f/16) to ensure everything from the foreground to the background is in focus.
- **Low Light Conditions:** A wide aperture allows more light into the camera, helping you capture properly exposed images in dim environments without increasing ISO too much.

Aperture Tips:

- **Bokeh Effect:** Use a wide aperture (f/1.8–f/2.8) to create a pleasing **bokeh** effect, where the background is blurred out, and the subject is sharply in focus.
- **Use a Tripod for Small Apertures:** When using narrow apertures (like f/16 or smaller) in low light, consider using a tripod to avoid camera shake.

How ISO, Shutter Speed, and Aperture Work Together: The Exposure Triangle

ISO, shutter speed, and aperture form the **exposure triangle**, where each setting affects the others:

- **ISO:** Controls sensitivity to light. A higher ISO allows shooting in lower light but introduces noise.
- **Shutter Speed:** Determines how long the sensor is exposed to light. A faster shutter speed is ideal for fast-moving subjects, while slower speeds capture motion blur or long exposure effects.
- **Aperture:** Controls how much light enters the camera and affects the depth of field. A wider aperture (low f-number) lets in more light and creates a shallow depth of field, while a smaller aperture (high f-number) reduces the light and increases depth of field.

By adjusting these three settings, you can control both the exposure (brightness) of your images and the **creative effects** in your photography.

Practical Examples

- **Well-lit Scene (Outdoor daylight):**
    - ISO: 100–200
    - Shutter Speed: 1/500s or faster (to freeze motion)
    - Aperture: f/5.6–f/8 (for sharp focus)
- **Indoor Low Light:**
    - ISO: 800–1600
    - Shutter Speed: 1/60s or slower (may need a tripod)
    - Aperture: f/2.8–f/4 (to allow more light)
- **Night Photography (Stars or city lights):**
    - ISO: 1600–3200 (higher ISO to avoid underexposure)
    - Shutter Speed: 10–30s (for long exposure)
    - Aperture: f/2.8–f/5.6 (wide aperture for light capture)

Understanding **ISO, shutter speed**, and **aperture** is essential for achieving the right exposure and creative control over your images. These three settings work together as the **exposure triangle**, where adjustments to one affect the others.

By mastering how each of these elements influences your photos, you'll be able to take full control over your shots, whether you're capturing fast-moving subjects, low-light scenes, or creating beautiful artistic effects.

5.2 Metering Modes and Exposure Compensation

Understanding metering modes and exposure compensation is crucial for achieving the desired exposure in different shooting scenarios. The Nikon D7500 offers various metering modes and an easy-to-use exposure compensation feature to help you take control of how light is measured and adjust exposure levels when necessary.

1. Metering Modes: How the Camera Measures Light

Metering modes determine how the camera measures the light in a scene to calculate the optimal exposure. The Nikon D7500 offers several metering modes, each suited for different types of scenes. These modes control how the camera evaluates the light and sets the exposure for the final image.

A. Matrix Metering

- **Description:** Matrix metering is the default and most commonly used metering mode. The camera evaluates the entire scene by dividing it into several zones. It takes into account factors such as brightness, contrast, and colours to determine the correct exposure.

- **Best for:** General photography, landscapes, portraits, and well-lit scenes.

- **Advantages:** Provides a balanced exposure by considering the whole scene, making it ideal for most situations.

B. Centre-Weighted Metering

- **Description:** In this mode, the camera meters light based on the central portion of the frame, but also considers the surrounding areas. The central area is given more priority, and the exposure is based on that region.

- **Best for:** Portraits, subjects with a central focus, or scenes where the subject is more important than the surrounding light.

- **Advantages:** Useful when the subject is in the centre of the frame and you want to ensure they are properly exposed, even if the surrounding areas are brighter or darker.

C. Spot Metering

- **Description:** Spot metering evaluates light from a very small area (usually 1-2% of the frame, typically the centre). This mode measures the brightness in that small area and adjusts the exposure accordingly.

- **Best for:** High-contrast scenes, where you need precise control over the exposure of a specific subject or area, such as when photographing a subject against a bright background.

- **Advantages:** Allows precise control when exposing for a specific point of interest in the frame (e.g., an individual's face against a bright sky).

D. Highlight-Weighted Metering (Available in some Nikon models)

- **Description:** Highlight-weighted metering gives priority to the brightest areas of the scene to prevent overexposure in highlights, such as in scenes with bright light sources or snow.

- **Best for:** High-contrast scenes with bright highlights, like shooting in bright sunlight, snow, or backlit subjects.

- **Advantages:** Helps preserve detail in the brightest parts of an image and prevents overexposure.

2. Exposure Compensation: Fine-Tuning Exposure

Exposure compensation allows you to manually adjust the exposure level when you feel the automatic metering might not produce the desired results. By dialing in exposure compensation, you can make the image brighter (overexpose) or darker (underexpose) to suit your creative intent.

How Exposure Compensation Works:

- **Positive Exposure Compensation (+):** Increases the exposure, making the image brighter. This is useful in situations where the camera underexposes the scene, such as when photographing a subject against a very bright background.

- **Negative Exposure Compensation (-):** Decreases the exposure, making the image darker. This is helpful when the camera overexposes the scene, like when photographing a white subject in bright light.

How to Adjust Exposure Compensation on the Nikon D7500:

1. Press the **Exposure Compensation button** (it's usually marked with a "+/-" symbol).
2. While holding down the button, turn the **main command dial** to adjust the exposure level.
3. The **exposure compensation scale** will appear in the viewfinder and on the LCD screen, showing the adjustments from -5 to +5.
4. Release the button to lock in your exposure compensation setting, and take the shot.

When to Use Exposure Compensation:

- **Backlit Subjects:** If you are photographing a subject against a bright light source, the camera may underexpose the subject (e.g., silhouette effect). Increase the exposure (+) to brighten the subject.

- **Snowy or Bright Scenes:** If the camera is metering for a bright scene (like snow), it may underexpose the image. Increase the exposure (+) to prevent the snow from looking gray.

- **Low-light Situations:** In dark environments, you may want to increase exposure (+) to brighten the image if it's too dark. However, be cautious of noise if ISO is too high.

- **Subjects with Large Dark Areas:** If your scene contains a lot of dark areas, the camera may overexpose the highlights. In such cases, you may want to decrease exposure (-) to avoid overexposing lighter parts of the scene.

3. Understanding the Exposure Triangle with Metering Modes and Compensation

While metering modes help you determine the exposure based on light measurement, exposure compensation lets you override the camera's automatic exposure settings for more creative control. These tools work in conjunction with **ISO, shutter speed**, and **aperture** to achieve the desired exposure.

- **Metering Modes:** Choose a metering mode that fits the scene to give the camera a better understanding of how to set exposure.
- **Exposure Compensation:** Adjust the exposure further to fine-tune the brightness or darkness of your image based on how the camera's metering mode evaluates the light.

By mastering both **metering modes** and **exposure compensation**, you'll have more control over your exposure and be able to get the results you want, regardless of the lighting conditions.

Practical Examples of Metering Modes and Exposure Compensation

- **Scene with a Subject in Front of a Bright Background (Backlighting):**
  - **Metering Mode:** Spot Metering (measuring light on the subject's face).
  - **Exposure Compensation:** Increase exposure (+) to brighten the subject's face.
- **Landscape Photography (Wide Scene with Different Lighting Levels):**
  - **Metering Mode:** Matrix Metering (evaluating the entire scene).
  - **Exposure Compensation:** Neutral or no compensation, unless the scene is overly dark or bright.
- **Subject in a Dimly Lit Room (Indoor Portrait):**
  - **Metering Mode:** Centre-weighted Metering (measuring light in the canter).
  - **Exposure Compensation:** Increase exposure (+) to compensate for the dim lighting.
- **Bright Snow Scene:**
  - **Metering Mode:** Matrix Metering or centre-weighted Metering.
  - **Exposure Compensation:** Increase exposure (+) to prevent the snow from appearing gray or underexposed. Metering modes and exposure compensation are essential tools for achieving the desired exposure in different photographic situations. By understanding how each metering mode works and how to adjust exposure compensation, you can ensure that your photos are properly exposed, regardless of the lighting conditions. Whether you're dealing with backlighting, high-contrast scenes, or low-light environments, mastering these features will give you more creative freedom and control over your images.

5.3 Using HDR and Bracketing

The Nikon D7500 offers powerful features like High Dynamic Range (HDR) and Exposure Bracketing that enable you to capture images with enhanced detail in both the brightest and darkest areas of a scene. These features are especially useful for high-contrast scenes or situations where traditional metering might not be able to capture the full range of light in a scene.

1. High Dynamic Range (HDR) on the Nikon D7500

HDR photography is a technique used to merge multiple images with different exposures to create a final image that captures a wider range of light, from highlights to shadows.

The Nikon D7500 automatically combines multiple exposures to create a balanced image with more detail in the highlights and shadows.

How HDR Works:

When you activate HDR, the camera captures two or more images at different exposures—one underexposed, one correctly exposed, and one overexposed. These images are then combined into a single image that has better detail in both bright and dark areas.

Steps to Use HDR on the Nikon D7500:

Activate HDR:

Press the **Menu** button.

Navigate to the **Shooting Menu** (camera icon).

Select **HDR (High Dynamic Range)**.

Set the **HDR** option to **On**.

Set the HDR Effect (Optional):

Choose between different HDR effect levels: **Low**, **Normal**, or **High**. The **High** setting will apply the most noticeable HDR effect.

Take the Shot:

Frame your subject and press the shutter button. The camera will automatically take multiple exposures and combine them into one final HDR image.

Review the Image:

The result should have enhanced detail in both the highlights and shadows, with smoother transitions in lighting.

When to Use HDR:

High-contrast scenes: Such as landscapes with a bright sky and dark foreground, or subjects backlit by a strong light source.

Indoor photography: For scenes with windows where the outside light is much brighter than the interior.

Scenes with both bright and dark areas: To ensure you capture details in both highlights and shadows.

2. Exposure Bracketing on the Nikon D7500

Exposure bracketing is a technique where the camera automatically takes a series of images at different exposures: one at the correct exposure, one overexposed, and one underexposed. This allows you to capture a range of exposures and choose the best one later or combine them to create an HDR image manually.

How Bracketing Works:

The Nikon D7500 offers exposure bracketing for capturing a series of images at multiple exposure levels. You can select how much you want the exposures to vary (e.g., 1 EV, 2 EV) between shots.

Steps to Use Exposure Bracketing on the Nikon D7500:

Enable Bracketing:

Press the **Menu** button.

Go to the **Shooting Menu** and select **BKT (Bracketing)**.

Choose **Exposure** to enable exposure bracketing.

Set Bracketing Parameters:

Select the **bracketing steps** (such as +/- **1 EV, +/- 2 EV**).

Choose the number of exposures (usually three—one normal exposure and one each for overexposed and underexposed).

Capture the Bracketed Shots:

Once bracketing is set up, press the shutter button. The camera will automatically take the series of shots at different exposures.

Review and Process:

You can select the image with the best exposure, or you can combine the images manually in post-processing software (like Adobe Lightroom or Photoshop) to create an HDR image.

When to Use Bracketing:

Scenes with wide exposure variation: Such as bright skies and dark foregrounds in a landscape shot, or interiors with windows.

High-contrast lighting conditions: Like shooting in sunlight with dark shadows.

Situations requiring precise control: For more control over the exposure range when automatic HDR is not preferred.

3. Combining HDR and Bracketing

You can combine both **HDR and Exposure Bracketing** for even more control over your images. By enabling bracketing, the camera will capture multiple exposures, and then HDR mode can be used to merge those exposures into a high-dynamic-range image. This is particularly useful in extremely high-contrast scenes.

Steps to Combine HDR and Bracketing:

Enable Exposure Bracketing: Set up bracketing to capture multiple exposures.

Activate HDR Mode: Turn on HDR mode, ensuring the camera will merge the bracketed exposures into a single HDR image.

Capture the Bracketed Images: Take the shots, and the camera will combine them into one HDR image.

Practical Scenarios for HDR and Bracketing

Landscape Photography:

A sunset or sunrise, where the sky is very bright but the foreground is dark.

HDR: The camera merges the bright sky with the dark foreground.

Bracketing: You can manually adjust the exposures for even more precise control or use HDR mode after bracketing.

Interior Photography:

A room with windows allowing bright light to spill in.

HDR: To balance the indoor lighting with the outdoor bright sunlight.

Bracketing: To capture different exposures and combine them for an optimal result.

Architecture:

Photographing buildings or structures with both bright windows and darker interiors.

HDR: Combine different exposures to capture both bright and shadowed areas.

Bracketing: Use bracketing to ensure a wide exposure range and merge in post-processing.

By mastering HDR and Exposure Bracketing on the Nikon D7500, you can capture scenes with a wider dynamic range and ensure that details are preserved in both the brightest and darkest areas of your images. HDR mode automatically merges exposures for you, while bracketing gives you the flexibility to manually adjust exposure settings or combine shots in post-processing for greater control. Whether you're photographing landscapes, interiors, or architecture, these features provide valuable tools for achieving stunning results in challenging lighting conditions.

5.4 Continuous Shooting and Burst Mode

The Nikon D7500 offers Continuous Shooting and Burst Mode for capturing fast-moving subjects or action sequences. These modes allow you to take multiple shots in quick succession, giving you the best chance of capturing the perfect moment in high-speed situations, such as sports, wildlife, or events.

1. Continuous Shooting Mode

Continuous shooting allows you to take a series of images without having to press the shutter button multiple times. This is ideal for subjects that are in motion or when you want to ensure that you capture the perfect expression or action at the right moment.

How Continuous Shooting Works:

When you set the camera to continuous shooting mode, the shutter will fire repeatedly as long as you hold the shutter button down, taking multiple frames in quick succession.

Steps to Enable Continuous Shooting:

1. **Turn the Mode Dial to the appropriate mode:**
   - Select a shooting mode that supports continuous shooting, such as **P, S, A, M**, or **Auto**.

2. **Set Continuous Shooting Mode:**
   - Press the **AF-ON** button or the **Release Mode** dial (located on the top of the camera).
   - From the options displayed, choose **Continuous High** or **Continuous Low**.
     - **Continuous High (CH):** The camera will shoot at a higher frame rate, ideal for fast-moving subjects.
     - **Continuous Low (CL):** The camera will shoot at a slower rate for subjects that aren't moving as quickly.

3. **Capture Images:**
   - Hold down the shutter button. The camera will continue taking shots until you release the button or the memory buffer fills up.

4. **Review the Shots:**
   - After releasing the shutter button, review the sequence of images you've captured to ensure you captured the perfect moment.

When to Use Continuous Shooting:

- **Sports Photography:** To capture fast action, such as athletes in motion, and select the best frame from a burst.
- **Wildlife Photography:** For capturing animals in motion, where it's difficult to predict the exact moment of the shot.
- **Events and Performances:** To capture fleeting moments, such as facial expressions, gestures, or specific moments in action.

2. Burst Mode

Burst mode is a more advanced setting that allows the camera to take a series of shots in rapid succession, making it perfect for fast-moving subjects or when you want to shoot at high frame rates. The Nikon D7500 can shoot up to 8 frames per second (fps) in **Continuous High (CH)** mode, which is ideal for sports or action photography.

How Burst Mode Works:

In burst mode, the camera will shoot multiple frames in rapid succession. It can capture several frames per second, allowing you to freeze the action in a high-speed situation.

Steps to Use Burst Mode:

1. **Set the Camera to Continuous High (CH) Mode:**
   - Set your camera to **Continuous High** (CH) mode for the highest burst rate.

2. **Choose a Shutter Speed:**
   - In burst mode, it's important to use a fast shutter speed to avoid motion blur in fast-moving subjects. The faster the shutter speed, the sharper the images will be.
   - For action shots, use shutter speeds around **1/500** to **1/2000** depending on the speed of the subject.

3. **Hold Down the Shutter Button:**
   - Once you've composed the shot, press and hold the shutter button to begin the burst.
   - The camera will take multiple frames, allowing you to choose the best shot later.

4. **Check Buffer Capacity:**
   - The Nikon D7500 has a buffer that temporarily stores the images before they are written to the memory card. If you're shooting continuously, ensure the buffer doesn't fill up, as it will slow down the frame rate.

5. **Post-processing:**
   - Review the burst sequence and choose the best image from the series. You can also create action sequences or time-lapses from the burst shots.

When to Use Burst Mode:

- **High-speed Sports:** Ideal for capturing fast-moving athletes, cars, or any fast-paced action.
- **Wildlife in Motion:** Perfect for capturing birds in flight, running animals, or fast-moving insects.
- **Dramatic Action Shots:** Great for events like concerts, performances, or any scene where split-second timing is crucial.

3. Frame Rate and Buffer Considerations

The Nikon D7500 has impressive burst capabilities with a high frame rate of up to **8 fps** in **Continuous High (CH)** mode. However, keep in mind that the **buffer size** can limit the number of shots you can take before the camera slows down to clear the buffer.

Frame Rate and Buffer Performance:

- **Continuous High (CH):** Up to 8 frames per second for fast action shots.
- **Continuous Low (CL):** Typically around 6 frames per second, which is suitable for slower action or subjects.
- **Buffer Limits:** The buffer holds a limited number of frames, so after shooting several images, the camera might slow down to process the photos before you can shoot again. You can monitor this through the **frame counter** displayed in the camera's viewfinder or LCD.

Maximizing Burst Performance:

- Use **high-speed SD cards** with fast write speeds to prevent the buffer from filling up quickly. Cards with UHS-I or UHS-II speeds are ideal for continuous shooting.

- If shooting RAW files, consider switching to JPEG if you need more shots in the burst sequence, as JPEG files take up less space in the camera's buffer.

4. Tips for Successful Continuous Shooting and Burst Mode

- **Keep the Camera Steady:** Use a fast shutter speed and a stable shooting position to avoid camera shake. A tripod or monopod may help in some situations, although it can limit mobility.

- **Pre-focus on the Subject:** For fast-moving subjects, it's helpful to pre-focus on the area where you expect the action to take place. This will allow the camera to track the subject more effectively.

- **Use Autofocus Tracking:** Use **Continuous AF (AF-C)** to keep your subject in focus while it moves. You can also select a specific autofocus area (like **Dynamic Area AF**) to ensure the camera tracks the subject accurately.

- **Burst Duration:** If you're shooting an extended burst, make sure to take breaks to let the camera cool down and clear the buffer, especially when shooting in high-speed mode.

Continuous Shooting and Burst Mode on the Nikon D7500 are powerful tools for capturing fast action, motion, and fleeting moments. Whether you're photographing sports, wildlife, or events, these modes allow you to take multiple shots in quick succession, giving you the best chance to capture the perfect moment. By understanding how to set up and optimize continuous shooting and burst mode, you can enhance your action photography and never miss a shot again.

CHAPTER SIX
VIDEO RECORDING

6.1 Video Quality Settings

The Nikon D7500 offers impressive video capabilities, making it a powerful tool for both amateur and professional videographers. With 4K UHD recording, full HD options, and various frame rates, the camera provides flexibility in choosing the best video quality settings for your needs. Here's an overview of the video settings on the Nikon D7500, including resolution, frame rate, and compression options.

1. Video Resolution and Frame Rate Options

The Nikon D7500 allows you to record videos at different resolutions and frame rates, depending on the level of detail and smoothness you need.

4K UHD (3840 x 2160)

- **Frame Rate Options:** 30p, 25p, 24p
- **Bitrate:** High-quality 4K UHD video with a bitrate that ensures crisp, detailed video.
- **Use Cases:** Ideal for cinematic video production or when you need the highest video resolution.

Full HD (1920 x 1080)

- **Frame Rate Options:**
    - **60p (Progressive)**
    - **50p**
    - **30p**
    - **25p**
    - **24p**
- **Bitrate:** Full HD offers a lower bitrate compared to 4K, but still delivers excellent video quality suitable for most video projects.
- **Use Cases:** Full HD is great for general video recording, including vlogging, YouTube videos, and social media content.

HD (1280 x 720)

- **Frame Rate Options:**
    - **60p (Progressive)**
    - **50p**
- **Use Cases:** Best for lower file sizes or when you need to save on storage space. Suitable for streaming or when 4K/Full HD isn't necessary.

2. Video Compression Options

The Nikon D7500 provides different video compression settings that balance quality and file size.

MOV Format

- **Compression Type:** H.264/MPEG-4 AVC
- **Bitrate:** High compression with minimal loss in quality.
- **Use Cases:** The MOV format is common for professional video editing, especially for workflows using Final Cut Pro or Adobe Premiere.

MP4 Format

- **Compression Type:** H.264/MPEG-4 AVC
- **Bitrate:** MP4 offers a smaller file size with relatively high quality, making it easier for sharing videos online.
- **Use Cases:** Ideal for general-purpose video recording, including online uploads, and when you need a smaller file size for quick sharing.

3. Autofocus in Video Recording

The Nikon D7500 features **Full-time Autofocus (AF)** during video recording, which allows for smooth transitions as you track moving subjects.

AF Modes for Video:

- **AF-F (Full-time Servo AF):** Continuous autofocus throughout the video. This is ideal for static subjects or when you're shooting in controlled conditions.
- **AF-S (Single AF):** Focus locks once, and you may need to manually adjust focus if the subject moves out of the frame.
- **Manual Focus (M):** This option allows you to control focus manually for precision, useful for cinematic shots or when autofocus may not be effective.

4. Audio Settings for Video

Good audio quality is just as important as video quality. The Nikon D7500 includes built-in microphones and a 3.5mm microphone jack for external microphones.

Built-in Microphone:

- The built-in microphone captures audio in stereo, but it may pick up camera noise or wind. You can adjust the sensitivity of the internal microphone through the menu.

External Microphone:

- For higher audio quality, you can attach an external microphone using the **3.5mm microphone input**. External microphones provide better control over sound quality, especially for professional recording.

Audio Levels:

- **Manual Audio Level Control:** You can manually adjust the microphone input sensitivity in the camera's settings to prevent distortion or overloading.
- **Wind Noise Reduction:** Turn this feature on to minimize wind noise if you're shooting outdoors.

5. Frame Rate Considerations and Slow Motion

The frame rate of your video affects how smooth the playback appears and whether you can create slow-motion effects.

Slow Motion Video:

- **Full HD at 60p or 50p**: When recording at a higher frame rate (e.g., 60p), you can slow down the footage in post-production to create smooth slow-motion effects.
- **4K UHD**: Slow-motion is not available at 4K resolution in this camera, but Full HD at high frame rates can provide similar results.

6. Video Exposure Settings

Just like still photography, exposure plays a critical role in video quality.

Manual Exposure:

- You can manually control **shutter speed**, **aperture**, and **ISO** to fine-tune exposure for video recording.
    - **Shutter Speed:** Use the **double frame rate rule** for natural motion. For example, when recording at 30p, set your shutter speed to **1/60**.
    - **Aperture:** Adjust the aperture for depth of field. A wider aperture (lower f-number) creates a shallower depth of field, while a smaller aperture (higher f-number) increases depth of field.
    - **ISO:** Adjust ISO to control exposure, but keep it as low as possible to avoid noise in low-light situations.

Auto Exposure:

- The camera also offers automatic exposure settings for video, but this may cause exposure changes during recording if the lighting conditions change.

7. Time-Lapse and Interval Shooting

The Nikon D7500 also allows you to create time-lapse videos by using the **interval shooting** mode, which takes a series of photos at specified intervals and then compiles them into a video sequence.

Setting Up Time-Lapse:

1. Go to the **Menu**, navigate to **Shooting Menu**, and select **Time-lapse Photography**.
2. Set the interval between shots and the total number of shots.
3. The camera will take the photos automatically, and you can compile them into a video.

8. Video Settings Summary

Setting	Option	Use Case
Resolution	4K UHD (30p, 25p, 24p), Full HD (60p, 50p)	High-quality video for various purposes
Compression	MOV (H.264/MPEG-4), MP4 (H.264/MPEG-4)	MOV for professional editing, MP4 for sharing
Autofocus	AF-F, AF-S, Manual Focus	AF for moving subjects, Manual for precision
Audio	Built-in mic, 3.5mm external mic input	High-quality audio capture with external mics
Frame Rate	30p, 25p, 24p, 60p, 50p	Smooth video playback and slow-motion
Shutter Speed	1/60 for 30p, adjust for other frame rates	For proper exposure and natural motion
ISO and Aperture	Manual control	Adjust for desired exposure and depth of field
Time-Lapse	Interval shooting	For creating time-lapse videos

The Nikon D7500 is a versatile camera for both stills and video, offering a range of high-quality video settings. With 4K UHD recording, multiple frame rates, manual exposure controls, and advanced autofocus options, it's a great choice for videographers looking to create cinematic video content. Whether you're shooting a vlog, short film, or time-lapse, the D7500's video capabilities give you flexibility and creative control over your footage.

6.2 Recording Movies

The Nikon D7500 offers a range of features that make it an excellent choice for recording high-quality videos. Whether you're shooting in 4K UHD, Full HD, or using the camera's time-lapse feature, the camera provides versatile tools for videographers. Below is a detailed guide on how to set up and record movies on the Nikon D7500.

1. Preparing the Camera for Movie Recording

Before you start recording, ensure that your camera is set up for optimal video performance.

Insert the Memory Card

- Insert a compatible **SD card** with sufficient capacity and write speed to handle video files. **UHS-I** or **UHS-II** SD cards are recommended for smoother performance.

Charge the Battery

- Ensure that your battery is fully charged to prevent the camera from turning off unexpectedly during recording.

2. Setting the Mode for Video Recording

To begin recording movies, you need to set the camera to the appropriate video mode.

Activate Movie Mode:

1. **Turn on the Camera** and set the mode dial to the **Movie Camera Icon** (the video camera symbol) or any of the shooting modes that support video, such as **P, S, A,** or **M**.
2. The camera will automatically switch to movie recording mode when in these modes, allowing you to record video.

3. Adjusting Video Settings

Before recording, you can adjust settings for optimal video quality.

Video Resolution and Frame Rate:

- Go to the **Menu > Shooting Menu > Movie Settings** to select the desired resolution and frame rate.
    - **4K UHD (3840 x 2160)** at 30p, 25p, or 24p for high-quality video.
    - **Full HD (1920 x 1080)** at 60p, 50p, 30p, 25p, or 24p for general video recording.
    - **HD (1280 x 720)** for lower-resolution video with smaller file sizes.

Choose Compression Format:

- In the **Movie Settings**, choose **MOV** or **MP4** format. MOV is better for professional editing, while MP4 is more suitable for uploading to social media.

Autofocus Mode:

- Set the camera to **AF-F (Full-time Servo AF)** for continuous autofocus during video recording.
- Alternatively, set it to **Manual Focus (M)** for full control over focus adjustments during recording.

Audio Settings:

- For better sound quality, you can use an external microphone via the **3.5mm microphone input**. If you're using the built-in microphone, adjust the **microphone sensitivity** in the audio settings.
- Enable **Wind Noise Reduction** if shooting outdoors.

4. Recording Movies

Once your settings are configured, you can begin recording.

Start Recording:

1. Press the **Movie Record Button** (located next to the shutter button or on the back of the camera, depending on the model).

2. The camera will begin recording video in the selected resolution and frame rate.

3. While recording, the **red record indicator** will appear on the screen or in the viewfinder to indicate that the camera is capturing footage.

Focus During Recording:

- If using **AF-F**, the camera will automatically focus on the subject, even if it moves.
- If using **Manual Focus**, adjust the focus ring on the lens to achieve the desired sharpness.

Monitoring Audio:

- During recording, you can monitor the audio levels on the camera's screen. Adjust the external microphone's volume or sensitivity through the **Audio Level** menu.

5. Stopping the Movie Recording

Once you're done recording, stop the movie by pressing the **Movie Record Button** again.

Post-Recording:

- You can review the recorded video on the camera's LCD screen by pressing the **Playback Button**.
- Use the **Thumbnail Button** to view the video in full-screen mode or scrub through it.

6. Additional Recording Features

Time-Lapse Video:

- The Nikon D7500 supports **Time-Lapse Recording**, which allows you to capture a series of photos at set intervals and convert them into a video. To set up time-lapse:

    1. Go to the **Menu > Shooting Menu > Time-lapse Photography**.
    2. Set the **interval** (e.g., 1 second, 10 seconds) and the **total number of shots**.
    3. The camera will automatically take photos, and you can compile them into a video.

Slow Motion Recording:

- For slow-motion effects, record at higher frame rates, such as **Full HD 60p** or **50p**, and then slow down the footage in post-processing.

7. Video Exposure Control

Proper exposure is essential for great video. The Nikon D7500 allows manual control over key exposure settings during video recording.

Shutter Speed:

- Set the shutter speed to **double the frame rate** (e.g., for 30p, use 1/60 shutter speed) for smooth, natural-looking motion.

Aperture:

- Adjust the **aperture** to control the depth of field. A wider aperture (f/1.4, f/2.8) will blur the background, while a smaller aperture (f/8, f/11) will keep more of the scene in focus.

ISO:

- Set the ISO manually to adjust the exposure in low-light conditions. A higher ISO allows more light but can introduce noise, so balance it with other settings.

Exposure Compensation:

- Use **Exposure Compensation** to adjust the brightness of the image. This is especially useful when shooting in challenging lighting conditions.

8. Reviewing and Editing the Movie

After recording, you can:

- Review the movie directly on the camera's LCD screen.
- Edit the video files in post-processing software like Adobe Premiere, Final Cut Pro, or DaVinci Resolve for color correction, audio enhancement, and more.

Recording movies with the Nikon D7500 is straightforward and provides you with plenty of control over video quality, autofocus, audio, and exposure. Whether you are filming in 4K UHD or Full HD, the camera's video capabilities offer professional-level performance for a variety of creative projects. With the ability to customize settings and use manual controls, you can create stunning videos with ease.

6.3 Using External Microphones

To enhance audio quality during video recording, the Nikon D7500 offers a 3.5mm microphone input that allows you to connect external microphones. This can significantly improve sound capture, especially when recording in noisy environments or requiring higher audio fidelity than the built-in microphone can provide.

Below is a detailed guide on how to set up and use external microphones with the Nikon D7500.

1. Choosing an External Microphone

Before you begin, select an appropriate external microphone based on your recording needs. Some common types of external microphones include:

Types of Microphones:

- **Lavalier Microphones (Clip-on mics):** Small, clip-on microphones that are ideal for interviews, vlogging, and hands-free use. They offer clear, close-range audio.

- **Shotgun Microphones:** Directional microphones that focus on capturing sound from a specific direction. These are great for outdoor shoots or environments with background noise.
- **Stereo Microphones:** Capture more natural, immersive sound, suitable for capturing ambient sounds and detailed audio.
- **Handheld Microphones:** Often used in interviews or event recording. These are typically more durable and offer good sound quality.

Choosing a Compatible Microphone:

- Look for microphones that have a **3.5mm TRS** (Tip-Ring-Sleeve) connector, which is compatible with the Nikon D7500's input.
- Ensure the microphone provides **manual gain control** (if needed), or select one that offers sufficient sensitivity levels for your recording environment.

2. Connecting the External Microphone

Once you have your microphone, you can connect it to the Nikon D7500:

1. **Turn Off the Camera:** It's always best to turn off the camera before connecting the microphone to avoid any potential damage.
2. **Plug in the Microphone:** Insert the **3.5mm microphone jack** from your external mic into the **microphone input** on the side of the camera.
3. **Turn on the Camera:** Once the microphone is connected, turn on the Nikon D7500.

3. Adjusting the Audio Settings

To ensure the best possible sound quality, configure the audio settings on the camera.

Manual Audio Level Control:

1. Go to the **Menu > Sound Settings > Microphone Sensitivity**.
2. Adjust the microphone sensitivity based on your external mic. You can choose **Auto**, which adjusts sensitivity automatically, or **Manual**, which allows you to set a custom audio level.
   - **Manual Sensitivity** is useful if you want to avoid distortion or noise in loud environments.
   - **Auto Sensitivity** is great for general recordings where automatic adjustment will work well.

Wind Noise Reduction:

- If you're shooting outdoors or in windy conditions, enable the **Wind Noise Reduction** option to minimize unwanted wind sounds that the microphone might pick up.
   - Go to **Menu > Sound Settings > Wind Noise Reduction** and turn it on.

Monitor Audio with Headphones:

- If your microphone has an audio output, you can plug in **headphones** to monitor the sound in real-time during recording.

- Use the **Headphone Output** on the camera (if available) or directly through your microphone (if it provides a headphone jack).

Audio Level Display:

- On the camera's **Live View screen**, you will see an **audio level meter** that displays the microphone input levels.
- Ensure the audio levels do not peak into the **red zone**, as this could cause distortion or clipping in the recorded audio. Adjust the sensitivity accordingly to keep the levels within an acceptable range.

4. Recording Audio with the External Microphone

Once your microphone is connected and settings are adjusted, you can start recording:

1. **Set the Camera to Movie Mode** by turning the mode dial to the **movie camera icon** or choose any other mode that supports video recording.
2. Press the **Movie Record Button** to start recording.
3. Monitor the audio levels during recording via the display or external headphones.
4. If necessary, pause and adjust the audio sensitivity or microphone placement to optimize sound

5. Troubleshooting Audio Issues

If you encounter any audio problems during or after recording, consider the following troubleshooting tips:

No Audio:

- Ensure that the microphone is properly connected to the camera's **3.5mm jack**.
- Check if the **microphone has a battery** (if it's battery-powered) and that it's turned on.
- Verify that the camera's **audio settings** are configured correctly (check that the sensitivity is not set too low).

Distorted or Low-Quality Audio:

- If using a **shotgun microphone**, make sure it is properly pointed towards the sound source.
- Check for **wind interference** and use **windshields** or enable the **wind noise reduction** feature.
- Ensure that the **audio levels** are not too high (which can cause distortion). Lower the sensitivity or use the manual gain control to fine-tune the audio.

Echo or Background Noise:

- If you hear an echo or unwanted background noise, try adjusting the **microphone's position** to face the sound source more directly.
- Consider using **directional microphones** for focused sound capture, or adjust the **gain levels** to reduce noise.

6. Additional Tips for Using External Microphones

- **Microphone Placement:** For optimal sound quality, place the microphone close to the sound source. For example, clip a lavalier microphone to the speaker's collar, or use a shotgun mic directly in front of the subject.

- **Monitor Audio Continuously:** Use headphones or the camera's audio display to continuously monitor the sound during recording. This helps catch issues like background noise, low levels, or distortion.

- **Use a Microphone Stand or Boom:** For more stable audio capture, use a **microphone stand** or **boom pole** for shotgun mics in interviews or field recordings.

Using an external microphone with the Nikon D7500 significantly enhances the audio quality of your video recordings. By selecting the right microphone, adjusting the camera's audio settings, and monitoring the sound during recording, you can ensure professional-grade audio for your projects. Whether you're capturing interviews, outdoor scenes, or music, the external mic options and controls on the Nikon D7500 provide flexibility and superior sound quality.

6.4 Time-Lapse and Slow-Motion Video

Nikon D7500 is equipped with powerful video recording features, including the ability to shoot Time-Lapse and Slow-Motion videos. These creative effects allow you to capture stunning footage, adding dynamic visual elements to your video projects. Below is a comprehensive guide on how to shoot both Time-Lapse and Slow-Motion videos using the Nikon D7500.

1. Time-Lapse Video on the Nikon D7500

Time-lapse photography allows you to capture a series of images at set intervals and then compile them into a video, creating a dramatic visual effect that compresses time. This feature is particularly effective for recording the movement of clouds, sunsets, busy streets, or nature.

Setting Up Time-Lapse Recording:

1. **Turn on the Camera:**
   - Ensure the camera is powered on and that you have a charged battery and sufficient memory space on your SD card.

2. **Select the Time-Lapse Mode:**
   - Press the **Menu** button and navigate to the **Shooting Menu**.
   - Scroll down to **Time-lapse Photography** and select it.

3. **Adjust Time-Lapse Settings:**
   - **Interval**: Set the interval at which the camera will take photos. For example, 1 second, 10 seconds, 30 seconds, etc. The longer the interval, the faster the time-lapse effect.
   - **Number of Shots**: Choose how many images the camera should take for the time-lapse. The more shots, the smoother the final video will be.

- o **Exposure Smoothing**: Enable this option to automatically adjust the exposure between frames for a smoother transition in lighting (e.g., when shooting a sunset).
- o **Interval Timer**: Adjust the interval timer (e.g., 1 second, 10 seconds) to control how frequently the camera captures each frame.

4. **Start Shooting:**
   - o Once the settings are configured, press **OK** to start the time-lapse sequence. The camera will automatically take pictures at the set intervals and store them on your SD card.
   - o You can monitor the progress of the time-lapse via the **LCD screen**.

5. **Creating the Time-Lapse Movie:**
   - o After capturing all the frames, go to the **Playback Menu**.
   - o Select **Time-lapse Movie** to convert the photos into a video.
   - o The camera will compile the series of photos into a time-lapse video at a frame rate of around **30 frames per second**.

2. Slow-Motion Video on the Nikon D7500

Slow-motion video allows you to capture fast-moving subjects at high frame rates and play them back at a slower speed. This effect is perfect for showing intricate details in action scenes, such as sports, water splashes, or the movement of objects.

Setting Up Slow-Motion Recording:

1. **Turn on the Camera:**
   - o Power on your Nikon D7500 and ensure the battery is charged and memory card has sufficient space for the high frame rate recording.

2. **Select Video Mode:**
   - o Set the camera to **Movie Mode** by turning the mode dial to the **movie camera icon** or choose any appropriate video recording mode (P, S, A, or M).

3. **Choose a High Frame Rate:**
   - o To achieve slow-motion, set the camera to a **high frame rate**. In the **Menu**, go to **Movie Settings** and select a high frame rate for slow-motion effects:
     - **Full HD (1920 x 1080)** at **60p, 50p** for smooth slow-motion.
     - You can also use **120p** (when available) to achieve an even slower effect in post-processing.

4. **Adjust Other Settings:**
   - o **Shutter Speed**: To maintain proper motion blur in slow-motion, set the **shutter speed to double the frame rate**. For example, if you're shooting at 60p, set the shutter speed to **1/120**.

- **Aperture**: Adjust the aperture to control depth of field. A smaller aperture (e.g., f/8) will keep more of the scene in focus.
- **ISO**: Set the ISO manually to adjust exposure. Be cautious of high ISO values, as they may introduce noise, especially in low light.

5. **Start Recording:**
    - Press the **Movie Record Button** to begin recording your slow-motion video. The high frame rate will capture more frames per second, allowing for detailed playback at a slower speed.
    - Monitor the audio and video via the **Live View screen** and adjust exposure settings as necessary.

6. **Playback and Post-Processing:**
    - After recording, you can view the slow-motion video on the camera's **LCD screen**.
    - Slow-motion is most noticeable when the video is played back in real-time, so you'll want to **slow down** the footage in post-production if necessary (especially if you recorded at **60p** or **120p**).
    - Use video editing software such as **Adobe Premiere Pro**, **Final Cut Pro**, or **DaVinci Resolve** to adjust the playback speed and create smoother slow-motion effects.

3. Combining Time-Lapse and Slow-Motion Effects

For advanced editing, you can also combine **Time-Lapse** and **Slow-Motion** techniques in post-production. By recording segments of time-lapse footage and segments of slow-motion footage, you can create visually captivating videos that show both the compression of time and the suspension of motion in a single project.

Tips for Combining Effects:

- **Transitions:** Use smooth transitions in editing software to seamlessly blend time-lapse and slow-motion segments.
- **Color Grading:** Enhance your video by adjusting the colors, contrast, and exposure to make the footage more striking.
- **Sound:** Slow-motion video may require adjustments to the audio. You can choose to mute or replace the audio in post-processing if necessary, especially since slow-motion may affect the original sound's pitch and quality

4. Tips for Great Time-Lapse and Slow-Motion Footage

Time-Lapse Tips:

- **Stabilize the Camera:** Use a tripod or other stabilizing gear to avoid unwanted movement during the time-lapse sequence.
- **Lighting Conditions:** Time-lapse works best with changing lighting conditions. Ensure you're shooting at times of day when light is changing, such as sunrise, sunset, or clouds moving.

- **Battery Life:** Time-lapse sequences can be long, so ensure your camera is connected to a stable power source or that your battery is fully charged.

Slow-Motion Tips:

- **High Frame Rate:** The more frames per second you record, the slower the effect will appear in the final video. Experiment with different frame rates to find the best look for your subject.
- **Lighting:** High frame rates require more light. Ensure you have adequate lighting to prevent the footage from appearing too dark or noisy.
- **Focus:** Fast-moving objects can be difficult to keep in focus. Use continuous autofocus (AF-C) or manually adjust the focus to maintain sharpness in the footage.

Both **Time-Lapse** and **Slow-Motion** video features on the Nikon D7500 offer powerful creative tools to enhance your video projects. Whether you're capturing the passage of time in a dramatic fashion or slowing down fast action for detailed analysis, the D7500 provides the flexibility and quality needed to achieve professional results. Experiment with different settings and techniques to get the most out of these features and elevate your videography.

CHAPTER SEVEN
PLAYBACK AND EDITING

7.1 Reviewing Photos and Videos

After capturing your photos and videos with the Nikon D7500, you'll want to review and analyse them to ensure they meet your expectations. The Nikon D7500 offers several features to help you efficiently review your media, check details, and make necessary adjustments.

Below is a detailed guide on how to review your photos and videos using the Nikon D7500.

1. Entering Playback Mode

To start reviewing your media, you'll need to enter **Playback Mode**:

- **Press the Playback Button**: This is located on the back of the camera, to the right of the **LCD screen** (represented by a **play symbol**).
- Once in **Playback Mode**, you'll be able to view the photos and videos you've captured.

2. Navigating Through Images and Videos

In **Playback Mode**, use the following controls to navigate through your photos and videos:

- **Use the Multi-Selector (D-pad) to scroll through images**:
  - **Up/Down Arrow**: Skip to the previous or next photo.
  - **Left/Right Arrow**: Jump to the previous or next photo/video.
- **Zoom In/Out**:
  - **Zoom In**: Press the + **button** to zoom in and examine details of the image. This is useful for checking focus, sharpness, or composition.
  - **Zoom Out**: Press the – **button** to zoom out and view the image in full-screen mode

3. Reviewing Photo Details

For photos, the Nikon D7500 provides several features to help you check for sharpness, exposure, and other key details:

Viewing the Histogram:

- The **histogram** is a graph that shows the distribution of light in your image, helping you assess exposure.
- **Activate the Histogram** by pressing the **Info button**. The histogram will appear alongside the image, showing the distribution of shadows, midtones, and highlights.

Zooming into the Image:

- After zooming in, use the **Multi-Selector** to move around the image and check the sharpness of specific areas, such as the eyes in a portrait or the details in a landscape shot.

Checking the Focus:

- After zooming in, check critical areas of the photo (e.g., eyes in portraits or focal points in landscapes) to ensure the image is properly focused.

Exif Data (Metadata):

- To review the settings used for a photo, such as **shutter speed**, **aperture**, and **ISO**, press the **Info button**. This will display a range of settings in addition to the image, allowing you to understand how the shot was captured

4. Reviewing Video Files

The process for reviewing videos on the Nikon D7500 is similar to that of photos, with a few additional features specific to video playback.

Video Playback:

- **Press the Play Button** to view your video. The video will play back on the LCD screen.
- Use the **Multi-Selector** to fast forward or rewind through the video, allowing you to review key sections.
- Press **OK** to pause or resume the video.

Frame-by-Frame Playback:

- While reviewing a video, you can advance one frame at a time by rotating the **Main Command Dial**. This is especially useful when reviewing fast-moving subjects to ensure you're capturing the right moment.

Viewing Audio Levels:

- During video playback, the camera will display an **audio level indicator** on the screen, which shows the volume levels captured by the built-in microphone or external microphone.
- Use this to check for any clipping or distortion in the audio.

5. Deleting Photos and Videos

If you find any photos or videos that you don't want to keep, the Nikon D7500 provides easy ways to delete them directly from **Playback Mode**:

1. **Select the File**: Use the Multi-Selector to highlight the photo or video you want to delete.
2. **Press the Trash Button**: Press the **Delete button** (trash can icon) to bring up the delete options.
3. **Confirm Deletion**: Select **Delete** or **Delete All** to remove the selected files from the memory card.

6. Rating Photos and Videos

To help organize and sort your media, the Nikon D7500 allows you to assign **ratings** to photos and videos:

1. **Press the OK button** when reviewing a photo or video.

2. Select **Rating** from the menu.
3. Choose a rating (1-5 stars) to assign to your media.
4. This rating can later be used to filter your photos when reviewing them on your computer.

7. Protecting Photos and Videos

To prevent accidental deletion, you can **protect** specific photos or videos:

1. In **Playback Mode**, highlight the photo or video you want to protect.
2. Press the **Protect button** (this may be accessible through the **Menu** or via a custom function).
3. Select **Protect** to lock the media and prevent it from being deleted.

8. Reviewing with the "Information" Button

The Nikon D7500 provides an **Info button** to display essential details about your photos and videos. When reviewing an image or video, pressing the **Info button** will cycle through various information overlays, such as:

- **File Info**: Displays file type, resolution, and size.
- **Exposure Info**: Shows shutter speed, aperture, and ISO settings.
- **Histogram**: Displays the histogram for assessing exposure.
- **Audio Levels (for video)**: Shows the sound levels during video playback.

9. Playback Settings

To customize the way media is displayed during playback, the Nikon D7500 provides various **Playback settings**:

1. **Image Review Settings**: Choose whether to automatically display the image right after you capture it.
2. **Playback Display Options**: Customize which details (like the histogram, grid, or exposure data) are shown during playback.
3. **Slideshow**: Use the **Slideshow function** to automatically cycle through your images in a set order, ideal for reviewing your shots in a more dynamic way or presenting them to others.

10. Transferring Media to Your Computer

After reviewing your photos and videos, you may want to transfer them to your computer for further editing or sharing.

1. **Connect the Camera via USB**: Use the provided USB cable to connect the Nikon D7500 to your computer. The camera will appear as a mass storage device.
2. **Transfer Files**: Open the folder where the camera files are stored and copy the images and videos to your computer.

Alternatively, you can remove the SD card from the camera and insert it into your computer's card reader for file transfer.

The Nikon D7500 offers a range of tools to review and assess your photos and videos effectively. With its ability to zoom in, check focus, review metadata, and view video footage with advanced controls, the D7500 ensures that you can analyze every shot thoroughly. By taking full advantage of these features, you can ensure the best possible results before moving on to editing or sharing your work.

7.2 Zooming In and Out on Playback

The Nikon D7500 offers an intuitive way to zoom in and out on images during playback, which is useful for checking image details like sharpness, focus, and exposure. Here's how to do it:

Zooming In During Playback

1. **Enter Playback Mode**:
   - Press the **Playback button** (the button with the play symbol) on the back of the camera to enter **Playback Mode**.

2. **Select the Image**:
   - Use the **Multi-Selector** (D-pad) to scroll through and highlight the image you want to zoom into.

3. **Zoom In**:
   - Press the **Zoom In button** (the **+ button** located on the back of the camera, near the Multi-Selector).
   - Each press of the **+ button** will zoom in further on the image, allowing you to examine details like the sharpness of specific areas.

4. **Move Around the Image**:
   - Once zoomed in, use the **Multi-Selector** to move around the image. This lets you view different areas of the image to check focus and details in specific sections.

Zooming Out During Playback

1. **Enter Playback Mode**:
   - If you're not already in **Playback Mode**, press the **Playback button** to review your images.

2. **Select the Image**:
   - Use the **Multi-Selector** to select the image you want to zoom out of.

3. **Zoom Out**:
   - Press the **Zoom Out button** (the **– button** located next to the Zoom In button).
   - Each press of the **– button** will zoom out, letting you return to the full image view or navigate to the next image more quickly.

Zooming In on Video Playback

- **Zooming** is not typically supported during video playback on the D7500.
- However, you can review specific parts of a video by pausing the video and using the **frame-by-frame** option (using the **Main Command Dial**) for detailed analysis.

Tips for Zooming During Playback

- **Use the Zoom function to check focus**: Zooming in helps you ensure your subject is in focus, especially for critical shots like portraits or macro photography.
- **Examine exposure and sharpness**: By zooming in, you can check for any exposure issues or soft spots in the image that might have been missed in the initial view.
- **Zoom to evaluate image quality**: When you zoom in on images with fine details, you can see how well the camera's sensor captured details and assess if you need to make adjustments for future shots.

Zooming in and out during playback on the Nikon D7500 provides an efficient way to evaluate your images. Whether you're checking focus, evaluating composition, or confirming exposure, this feature ensures you have the flexibility to thoroughly review your shots for the best possible results.

7.3 Retouching Images in Camera

The Nikon D7500 offers built-in retouching tools that allow you to enhance and adjust your images directly on the camera, without the need for external software. These tools are helpful for making quick adjustments and fine-tuning your photos while you're still on the go. Here's a guide on how to retouch images using the Nikon D7500:

1. Entering Retouch Mode

1. **Playback Mode**: First, enter **Playback Mode** by pressing the **Playback button** on the back of the camera.
2. **Select the Image**: Use the **Multi-Selector** (D-pad) to scroll through and select the image you want to retouch.
3. **Enter Retouch Menu**:
   - Press the **Menu button**.
   - Navigate to the **Retouch menu** under the **Playback Menu** (the icon looks like a pencil).

2. Available Retouching Options

The Nikon D7500 offers a variety of retouching options that can be applied to your photos. Here's a rundown of the available tools:

Basic Editing Options:

1. **Quick Retouch**:
   - This feature automatically adjusts the contrast and sharpness of your image to make it look more vibrant.

- **How to Use**: After selecting **Quick Retouch**, press **OK** to apply the effect.

2. **D-Lighting**:
   - D-Lighting enhances the shadows and highlights in your image, making it look better in high-contrast situations.
   - **How to Use**: Choose **D-Lighting** and select the level of enhancement (Low, Normal, or High) that you prefer.

3. **Color Balance**:
   - This tool allows you to adjust the color tone of your image, making it cooler or warmer.
   - **How to Use**: Select **Color Balance** and adjust the sliders to achieve the desired effect.

Creative Editing Tools:

1. **Filter Effects**:
   - The Nikon D7500 includes several **filter effects** that allow you to apply various artistic styles to your images.
   - Options include **Pop, Toy Camera, High Key, Low Key, and more**.
   - **How to Use**: Choose the filter effect, adjust intensity if needed, and press **OK** to apply.

2. **Trim (Cropping)**:
   - This option lets you crop the image to remove unwanted parts or to change the aspect ratio.
   - **How to Use**: Select **Trim**, choose the area you want to keep by adjusting the crop box, and press **OK** to apply the crop.

3. **Straighten Image**:
   - This tool helps correct any tilted images by straightening the horizon.
   - **How to Use**: Select **Straighten**, then rotate the image using the multi-selector until it is level. Press **OK** to apply.

4. **Monochrome (Black & White)**:
   - This option allows you to convert your image to black and white, with options for adjusting contrast and brightness.
   - **How to Use**: Select **Monochrome** and adjust the effect using the sliders.

Advanced Editing:

1. **Red-Eye Correction**:
   - If the flash caused red-eye in your portrait shots, this tool can automatically correct the red-eye effect.

- How to Use: Select **Red-Eye Correction**, then choose the eyes you want to correct. The camera will automatically adjust the red-eye.

2. **Filter Effects for Specific Areas (Soft Focus, Fisheye, etc.)**:
   - These tools let you apply specific filters like **Soft Focus** or **Fisheye** to certain areas of the image.
   - **How to Use**: Choose the filter, and you may be able to adjust the effect's strength and position.

3. Saving and Finalizing Changes

Once you've applied the desired retouching effect(s), you can:

1. **Save as New Image**:
   - After retouching, you'll be prompted to save the changes. You can either **overwrite** the original image or save it as a new file (retaining the original image).
   - **Choose "Save as New File"** if you want to keep the original intact.

2. **Exit Retouch Mode**:
   - After making your adjustments, you can exit the Retouch Menu by pressing the **Back button** or **Menu button**.

4. Tips for Effective Retouching

- **Avoid Over-Editing**: While the retouching tools are powerful, over-editing can lead to unnatural-looking images. Use subtle adjustments for the best results.
- **Use Multiple Tools**: You can combine tools, such as applying **D-Lighting** and then enhancing the **color balance**, to improve the overall look of your photo.
- **Compare Before and After**: Before saving your retouched image, compare it with the original to ensure the changes enhance your photo as intended.
- **Save a Copy**: Always opt to **save as a new file** when applying retouching, as it ensures your original photo is preserved.

The retouching options available on the Nikon D7500 provide a simple yet effective way to enhance your images without needing to transfer them to a computer. From adjusting exposure and contrast to applying creative filters and removing red-eye, the in-camera editing tools make it easy to refine your photos before sharing or printing them.

7.4 Deleting Files

The Nikon D7500 allows you to delete unwanted images or videos directly from the camera's memory card. Whether you want to free up space on your SD card or remove a mistake, here's a guide on how to delete files on your camera.

1. Enter Playback Mode

1. **Playback Mode**:
    - Press the **Playback button** (the button with the play symbol) located on the back of the camera.
    - This will display your most recent photos or videos on the screen.

2. Select the File to Delete

1. **Navigate Through Images**:
    - Use the **Multi-Selector** (the D-pad) to scroll through the images or videos.
    - Highlight the image or video you want to delete.
2. **Preview the File**:
    - Press the **OK button** to preview the selected file, if necessary, before deletion.

3. Delete a Single Image or Video

1. **Delete Option**:
    - With the image or video highlighted, press the **Delete button** (the **trash can icon**) on the back of the camera.
2. **Confirm Deletion**:
    - A prompt will appear on the screen asking, "Delete this image?"
    - Select **Delete** by pressing the **OK button** to confirm.
    - The image or video will be deleted from the memory card.

4. Delete Multiple Files (Batch Delete)

1. **Enter Menu for Multiple Deletions**:
    - In **Playback Mode**, press the **Menu button** to access the camera's menu.
2. **Navigate to Delete Option**:
    - Under the **Playback Menu**, scroll down and select **Delete** (or **Delete Multiple** in some menu versions).
3. **Select Files to Delete**:
    - Use the **Multi-Selector** to highlight and check the images or videos you want to delete. You can choose multiple files at once.

4. **Confirm Deletion**:
    - After selecting the files, press **OK** to confirm the deletion. A prompt will appear asking if you're sure about deleting these files.
    - Confirm by selecting **Delete**.

5. Delete All Files on the Memory Card

If you wish to delete **all files** on the memory card:

1. **Menu Navigation**:
    - Press the **Menu button** to open the menu system.
    - Navigate to the **Setup Menu** and select **Format**.
2. **Format Option**:
    - Select **Format** to erase all files on the memory card, including photos, videos, and any other data. This is a permanent action, so use it carefully.
3. **Confirm Format**:
    - The camera will prompt you to confirm that you want to format the memory card. Select **OK** to proceed, and all files will be erased.

6. Tips for Deleting Files

- **Be Careful**: Deleting images or videos is permanent, especially when using the "Format" option. Always double-check before confirming deletions.
- **Use "Delete All" for Emptying the Card**: If you're preparing your memory card for new shoots, consider formatting it instead of deleting individual files.
- **Review Before Deleting**: Make sure you're deleting the right image. The camera gives you an option to cancel the deletion, but once confirmed, it cannot be undone.

Deleting files on the Nikon D7500 is straightforward, whether you're removing a single image or clearing all files on your memory card. Just be sure to double-check before confirming deletions, as the action is irreversible, especially when formatting the card.

CHAPTER EIGHT
CUSTOMIZING CAMERA SETTINGS

8.1 Custom Menu Settings

The Nikon D7500 allows you to personalize the camera's settings through the Custom Menu. This feature enables you to customize various camera functions and fine-tune the settings to match your shooting style. Below is a guide on how to access and configure the Custom Menu Settings on the Nikon D7500.

1. Accessing the Custom Menu

1. **Enter Menu**:
   - Press the **Menu button** on the back of the camera to open the main menu.

2. **Navigate to Custom Settings**:
   - Use the **Multi-Selector** (D-pad) to scroll through the tabs at the top of the menu.
   - The **Custom Settings Menu** is marked with a **pencil icon** and is typically the **fifth** or **sixth** tab in the menu system.

2. Custom Menu Categories

The **Custom Settings Menu** offers various categories for customization. Here are some of the key settings you can adjust:

A. Autofocus (AF)

- **AF-C Priority Selection**:
   - Customize whether the camera will prioritize **focus** or **release** when shooting in **Continuous Autofocus (AF-C)** mode. This can be set to prioritize sharp focus or fast shutter release.

- **Focus Tracking with Lock-On**:
   - Adjust the tracking sensitivity and how the camera reacts to focus changes on moving subjects.

- **AF-Area Mode**:
   - Choose how the camera will select the focusing points: **Single-point AF**, **Dynamic-area AF**, or **3D-tracking**.

B. Exposure

- **Auto ISO Sensitivity Control**:
   - Set whether to allow the camera to adjust the **ISO** automatically in low-light conditions and at slow shutter speeds.

- **Exposure Delay Mode**:
  - Enable a short delay before the camera takes the shot to reduce camera shake, particularly when shooting at slow shutter speeds.
- **Flash Control**:
  - Customize flash settings, including whether the camera uses the built-in flash or external flash units, and the flash sync mode.

C. Buttons and Controls

- **Shutter Button AE-L**:
  - Set the **AE-L (Auto Exposure Lock)** function to be activated with the shutter button, or set it to a separate button for more precise control.
- **Function Button Settings**:
  - Customize the function buttons (**Fn, AE-L/AF-L**) to activate specific features like **ISO**, **White Balance**, or **Focus Mode**.
- **Display Brightness**:
  - Adjust the brightness level of the **LCD screen** and **viewfinder** for optimal visibility in different lighting conditions

D. Image Quality and Size

- **JPEG Compression**:
  - Choose the level of **JPEG compression** and adjust the **image quality** (Fine, Normal, Basic).
- **Raw File Size**:
  - Select the resolution of **RAW files** (Large, Medium, Small) to control file size and image quality.
- **Picture Control**:
  - Customize the **color, contrast, and sharpness** settings for different shooting styles (Standard, Neutral, Vivid, etc.).

E. Movie Settings

- **Movie Quality Settings**:
  - Customize video recording settings, such as **resolution** (4K, Full HD) and **frame rate** (30fps, 60fps).
- **Microphone Settings**:
  - Control the **microphone sensitivity** for movie recording, as well as **wind noise reduction** settings.

F. Viewfinder and LCD Settings

- **Viewfinder Display**:
  - Choose what information appears in the **viewfinder** (e.g., focus points, exposure settings).

- **Live View Display**:
  - Customize the **Live View** display to show grid lines, histograms, and other shooting aids.

- **Grid Display**:
  - Set a grid pattern to help with composition in both **Live View** and **Viewfinder** modes.

G. Focus and Shutter Settings

- **Shutter Release Button**:
  - Customize how the shutter button behaves, including options for **continuous shooting** and **focus priority**.

- **Focus Fine-Tuning**:
  - Adjust the fine-tuning of autofocus for different lenses to achieve precise focus, especially for macro or telephoto lenses.

3. Adjusting the Custom Settings

1. **Select the Option to Customize**:
   - Using the **Multi-Selector**, navigate through the options in the **Custom Settings Menu**.

2. **Make Adjustments**:
   - When you select a custom setting, the camera will often give you a range of options or a slider to adjust the setting.
   - For example, to change the **AF-C Priority**, you can choose between **Focus** or **Release** as the priority action.

3. **Save Settings**:
   - After making the desired adjustments, press the **OK button** to save the changes.

4. Resetting Custom Settings

If you want to return to the default factory settings for the **Custom Menu**, follow these steps:

1. **Enter Menu**:
   - Press the **Menu button** and navigate to the **Custom Settings Menu**.

2. **Choose Reset Option**:
   - Look for an option like **Reset Custom Settings** or **Reset All Settings**.

3. **Confirm Reset**:
    - Follow the on-screen instructions to reset the settings to the factory defaults.

5. Tips for Using Custom Settings

- **Use Custom Settings for Your Workflow**: Tailor the settings to match the type of photography you do most often (e.g., portrait, sports, landscape).

- **Test Settings Before Important Shoots**: Test your custom settings in different environments before using them in critical situations.

- **Create Presets for Quick Access**: You can assign frequently used settings to **function buttons** for faster access during shoots.

- **Fine-Tune Focus and Exposure**: Use custom settings to fine-tune the autofocus and exposure to match your specific needs, especially in challenging lighting conditions.

The Custom Menu Settings on the Nikon D7500 provide great flexibility and control over how the camera functions. By adjusting the settings to fit your personal preferences and shooting style, you can enhance your workflow and optimize the camera's performance for various types of photography.

8.2 Assigning Functions to Buttons

One of the great features of the Nikon D7500 is its ability to assign custom functions to the camera's buttons, making it easier to access frequently used settings quickly. This can enhance your shooting efficiency, allowing you to focus on capturing the moment rather than navigating through menus.

Here's a guide on how to assign functions to the buttons on the Nikon D7500:

1. Accessing the Customization Menu

1. **Enter the Menu**:
    - Press the **Menu button** on the back of the camera to open the main menu system.

2. **Navigate to the Custom Settings Menu**:
    - Using the **Multi-Selector**, scroll through the menu tabs at the top.
    - The **Custom Settings Menu** is usually indicated by a **pencil icon** and can typically be found as the **fifth** or ****sixth** tab.

3. **Go to the Buttons Customization Section**:
    - In the **Custom Settings Menu**, look for the section labeled **Controls** or **Button Functions**. This section allows you to assign functions to various camera buttons.

2. Choosing a Button to Customize

The Nikon D7500 offers several buttons that can be customized, including the **Fn** button, **AE-L/AF-L** button, and the **Sub-command dial**. Here's a breakdown of the buttons you can customize:

- **Fn (Function) Button**: Located on the front of the camera, this button can be assigned to frequently used settings like **ISO, White Balance, Focus Mode**, etc.

- **AE-L/AF-L Button**: Positioned on the back of the camera, this button is used to lock **exposure** and **autofocus**, but can be customized for other tasks.
- **Sub-command Dial**: Located near the shutter button, it can be assigned to control settings like **shutter speed**, **aperture**, or **exposure compensation**.
- **Multi-Selector**: The directional pad can be customized to control specific features, such as **focus points** or **drive modes**.
- **Movie Record Button**: You can assign other functions to the **movie record button** for quick access to settings or shooting modes.
- **Depth of Field Preview Button**: If you're not using this button for previewing the depth of field, you can assign it to control features like **HDR** or **flash** settings.

3. Customizing the Button Function

1. **Select the Button to Customize**:
   - In the **Button Functions** section, select the button you want to customize (e.g., **Fn button**).
2. **Choose the Function**:
   - After selecting the button, a list of available functions will appear. Some options might include:
     - **ISO Sensitivity**
     - **White Balance**
     - **Metering Mode**
     - **AF Mode**
     - **Focus Point Selection**
     - **Flash Control**
     - **Image Quality** (RAW, JPEG)
     - **Self-timer**
     - **Exposure Compensation**
3. **Assign the Function**:
   - Scroll through the list of functions and select the one you wish to assign to the button.
   - Press the **OK button** to confirm the selection.

4. Assigning Functions to Multiple Buttons

You can assign different functions to various buttons. For example:

- Assign **ISO sensitivity** to the **Fn button** for quick ISO adjustments.
- Set the **AE-L/AF-L button** to **focus point selection** to allow fast focusing changes.

- Customize the **Sub-command dial** to adjust **shutter speed** while shooting.

This customization can be particularly helpful when you need to access specific settings without taking your eyes off the scene.

5. Resetting Button Functions

If you want to reset the button functions to their default settings:

1. **Enter the Custom Settings Menu**.
2. **Navigate to the Button Function Reset Option**.
3. **Confirm Reset**:
   - Follow the on-screen instructions to reset all button functions to the factory defaults.

6. Tips for Assigning Functions

- **Prioritize Essential Functions**: Choose functions you adjust frequently, such as **ISO** or **focus mode**, and assign them to easily accessible buttons for faster adjustments.
- **Use for Quick Adjustments**: Assign the **Fn** button or **AE-L/AF-L** button to settings you need to change quickly, such as **exposure compensation** or **white balance**.
- **Create a Consistent Workflow**: Customize the buttons in a way that fits your shooting style, ensuring all essential controls are just a button press away.

Customizing the buttons on the Nikon D7500 is a great way to streamline your shooting process and make key settings more accessible. By assigning important functions to buttons like the **Fn** button and **AE-L/AF-L** button, you can adjust settings quickly and efficiently without taking your eyes off the subject. Experiment with different assignments to create a configuration that works best for you.

8.3 Configuring User Settings (U1, U2)

The Nikon D7500 offers two customizable user settings, **U1** and **U2**, that allow you to save and quickly recall your preferred camera settings for different shooting situations. This feature is perfect for photographers who need to switch between different setups (e.g., landscape, portrait, sports) without having to manually adjust all settings each time.

Here's a guide on how to configure and use **User Settings (U1, U2)** on the Nikon D7500:

1. Accessing the User Settings (U1, U2)

1. **Turn On the Camera**:
   - Make sure the camera is powered on.
2. **Set the Mode Dial to U1 or U2**:
   - The **U1** and **U2** settings are located on the **mode dial** at the top of the camera.
   - Turn the mode dial to **U1** or **U2** to access one of the custom user settings.

3. **Entering the Menu**:
    - If you want to adjust or save custom settings, press the **Menu button** to open the camera's menu system.

2. Configuring User Settings (U1, U2)

To configure **U1** or **U2** with your desired settings, follow these steps:

1. **Set the Camera to Your Preferred Settings**:
    - Manually adjust the camera settings to match your preferred configuration for shooting. This may include adjustments to:
        - **ISO**
        - **Shutter Speed**
        - **Aperture**
        - **White Balance**
        - **Focus Mode**
        - **AF Area Mode**
        - **Metering Mode**
        - **Drive Mode** (Continuous, Single, Self-timer)
        - **Image Quality (RAW/JPEG)**
        - **Flash Settings**
        - **Picture Control**
    - Set these values based on the type of photography you are doing (e.g., **U1** for landscape settings and **U2** for action or portrait shots).

2. **Save Your Settings to U1 or U2**:
    - Once your camera settings are configured, press the **Menu button**.
    - Navigate to the **Custom Settings Menu** (pencil icon) or the **Setup Menu**.
    - Look for the option labelled **Save User Settings** or **Save Settings to U1/U2**.
    - Select **U1** or **U2** and confirm that you want to save the current settings to that user slot.

3. Using User Settings (U1, U2)

After configuring your settings, switching between **U1** and **U2** is simple:

1. **Switch to U1 or U2 on the Mode Dial**:
    - To recall your customized settings, turn the **Mode Dial** to **U1** or **U2**.

- The camera will immediately load the settings you saved in that slot.

2. **Shoot with Your Pre-Set Configuration**:
    - Once you've switched to **U1** or **U2**, you can begin shooting with the settings you configured. This is ideal for quickly switching between setups without manually changing each setting.

4. Editing or Resetting User Settings

If you want to update or reset the settings stored in **U1** or **U2**, follow these steps:

1. **Change the Settings**:
    - Adjust the camera settings again, as needed (for example, for a different shooting scenario).

2. **Save New Settings**:
    - Once you've made the adjustments, go back to the **Menu** and choose **Save User Settings**.
    - Select either **U1** or **U2** to overwrite the previous configuration with the new settings.

3. **Reset User Settings**:
    - If you want to clear the settings in **U1** or **U2**, select **Reset Settings** in the **Menu**, which will return those slots to their default settings.

5. Tips for Using User Settings

- **Use for Different Shooting Styles**: Assign **U1** for one type of photography (e.g., landscapes, with specific aperture and ISO settings), and **U2** for another (e.g., fast action shots with different shutter speed and autofocus settings).

- **Keep It Simple**: Only save the settings you frequently change, so you can switch quickly between setups without diving into the menus.

- **Create a Quick Workflow**: Using **U1** and **U2** can streamline your shooting process, especially when you're shooting in varying conditions or need to switch setups between shots.

- **Experiment with Custom Configurations**: Test different settings for **U1** and **U2** to find out which setups work best for your specific photography needs.

User Settings (**U1** and **U2**) on the Nikon D7500 provide a powerful way to store and recall custom configurations for different types of photography. By setting up **U1** and **U2**, you can streamline your workflow and have immediate access to your preferred camera settings, whether you're switching from landscape to action shots or experimenting with different modes and configurations. This feature saves time and ensures you're always ready to shoot with optimal settings.

8.4 Customizing Autofocus

The autofocus (AF) system on the Nikon D7500 is highly customizable, offering a range of options that help you achieve sharp, precise focus in various shooting scenarios. Whether you're photographing fast-moving subjects, portraits, or landscapes, customizing your AF settings can significantly improve your results.

Here's a guide on how to customize the autofocus on the Nikon D7500:

1. Understanding the Autofocus System

The Nikon D7500 uses a **Multi-CAM 3500 II** autofocus sensor, which provides **51 AF points** with **15 cross-type sensors** for fast and accurate focusing. The system offers multiple AF modes and areas, each designed for specific situations.

Key Autofocus Settings:

- **AF-S (Single-Servo AF)**: Focuses once when you press the shutter button halfway. Ideal for stationary subjects.

- **AF-C (Continuous-Servo AF)**: Continuously adjusts focus while you hold the shutter button halfway. Perfect for moving subjects.

- **AF-A (Auto AF-S/AF-C)**: Automatically switches between AF-S and AF-C based on subject movement.

- **MF (Manual Focus)**: Allows you to manually adjust focus.

2. Configuring AF Mode

To choose the AF mode (AF-S, AF-C, or AF-A), follow these steps:

1. **Press the AF Mode Button**:
    - On the back of the camera, press the **AF Mode button** (located near the top-left corner).

2. **Select the Mode**:
    - Use the **Multi-Selector** or **Sub-command dial** to choose between:
        - **AF-S** for stationary subjects.
        - **AF-C** for moving subjects.
        - **AF-A** for automatic switching based on subject movement.

3. **Confirm Your Selection**:
    - Once you've selected the mode, release the AF Mode button, and the setting will be applied.

3. Customizing AF Area Modes

The D7500 offers different **AF Area Modes**, allowing you to choose how the camera selects the focus points. These modes can be customized to suit different subjects and shooting conditions.

AF Area Modes:

- **Single Point AF**: Focuses using a single AF point (ideal for precise focusing on a specific area).
- **Dynamic Area AF**: Uses a group of AF points, which helps track moving subjects.
- **3D-Tracking**: Tracks a subject in the frame based on color and pattern, especially useful for fast-moving subjects.
- **Auto Area AF**: The camera automatically selects the AF points based on subject detection.
- **Group Area AF**: Uses a group of points to track subjects, providing better results for fast or erratic movement.

To customize the AF Area Mode:

1. **Press the AF Area Mode Button**:
    - Press the **AF Area Mode** button on the back of the camera.
2. **Select the Desired Mode**:
    - Use the **Multi-Selector** or **Sub-command dial** to choose the mode that best suits your shooting situation.
3. **Confirm Your Selection**:
    - Once selected, release the button, and the chosen AF area mode will be applied.

4. Customizing Focus Points

The Nikon D7500 allows you to manually select focus points, so you can focus exactly where you want in the frame.

To customize the focus point:

1. **Press the AF Area Mode Button**:
    - Press the **AF Area Mode button** and select **Single Point AF** or **Dynamic Area AF**.
2. **Use the Multi-Selector**:
    - After selecting the AF area mode, use the **Multi-Selector** to move the focus point to your desired location within the frame.
3. **Lock Focus**:
    - Press the **Shutter button halfway** or use the **AE-L/AF-L button** to lock focus on the selected point.

5. Fine-Tuning Autofocus with Custom Settings

For more precise control over the autofocus system, you can adjust certain settings in the **Custom Settings Menu** to tailor the autofocus to your preferences. These settings can help optimize focus speed and accuracy for various subjects and shooting conditions.

To Access Custom AF Settings:

1. **Press the Menu Button**:
   - Open the **Menu** and navigate to the **Custom Settings Menu** (pencil icon).

2. **Navigate to the Autofocus Section**:
   - Select **Autofocus** (AF) options within the menu to adjust settings such as **AF Fine-Tune, Focus Tracking Sensitivity**, and **AF-C Priority Selection**.

Key Custom Autofocus Settings:

- **AF Fine-Tune**: Allows you to adjust the autofocus to compensate for minor focus errors (ideal for lenses that may require calibration).
- **Focus Tracking Sensitivity**: Controls how quickly the autofocus system adjusts when the subject moves in or out of focus. A higher sensitivity results in faster tracking.
- **AF-C Priority Selection**: Allows you to set the priority between focus accuracy and shutter release during continuous autofocus. This can be set to either **Release** or **Focus**.

6. Assigning AF Functions to Buttons

You can also assign autofocus functions to customizable buttons on the camera for quicker access. For example, you might want to assign **AF-On** to the **AE-L/AF-L button** to activate autofocus independently of the shutter button.

To assign AF functions to buttons:

1. **Press the Menu Button** and navigate to **Custom Settings Menu**.
2. **Select Controls**.
3. **Choose Button Customization**.
4. **Assign AF Functions** to your desired buttons (e.g., **AF-On** or **AF-L**).

7. Tips for Customizing Autofocus

- **Use AF-C for Moving Subjects**: When photographing moving subjects, use **AF-C** (Continuous AF) along with **Dynamic Area AF** or **3D Tracking** for better tracking performance.
- **Single Point AF for Precision**: For still subjects or when you need precise control over the focus point, use **Single Point AF**.
- **Customize Focus Tracking Sensitivity**: Adjust the **Focus Tracking Sensitivity** if you're shooting fast-moving subjects, like sports, to fine-tune how the camera responds to subject changes.
- **Use Back-Button Autofocus**: Assign the **AF-On** function to the **AE-L/AF-L button** for back-button autofocus, which allows you to separate focusing and shutter release for more control.

- **Regularly Check AF Fine-Tune**: If you notice that your images are slightly out of focus, particularly with specific lenses, you may need to use the **AF Fine-Tune** feature to calibrate the focus.

Customizing the autofocus on your Nikon D7500 gives you greater control over focusing, ensuring you can achieve sharp, accurate results for any type of photography. Whether you're capturing fast action, portraiture, or still life, customizing your AF settings — from choosing the right AF mode to adjusting tracking sensitivity — will help you get the best out of your camera. Experiment with different AF modes and fine-tuning options to discover the settings that work best for your style of shooting.

CHAPTER NINE
CONNECTIVITY

9.1 Setting Up Wi-Fi and Bluetooth

The Nikon D7500 has built-in Wi-Fi and Bluetooth capabilities, which allow you to wirelessly transfer images to your smartphone or tablet, remotely control the camera, and share photos directly to social media. Here's a step-by-step guide on how to set up and use the Wi-Fi and Bluetooth features on your D7500:

1. Setting Up Wi-Fi on the Nikon D7500

Wi-Fi allows you to transfer photos and videos from the camera to a smartphone or computer and even control the camera remotely.

Step 1: Enable Wi-Fi on the Camera

1. **Press the Menu Button**:
    - Press the **Menu** button to open the camera's settings.
2. **Navigate to the Wi-Fi Settings**:
    - In the **Setup Menu** (wrench icon), scroll down to find **Wi-Fi** or **Network Settings**.
    - Select **Wi-Fi** or **Wi-Fi Settings** to enable the feature.
3. **Enable Wi-Fi**:
    - Turn **Wi-Fi** to **On**. The camera will now be ready to connect to a device via Wi-Fi.

Step 2: Pair the Camera with Your Smartphone

1. **Install the Nikon SnapBridge App**:
    - Download the **Nikon SnapBridge** app from the **App Store** (iOS) or **Google Play** (Android) if you haven't already. This app will allow you to connect your smartphone to the camera and transfer images wirelessly.
2. **Open the SnapBridge App**:
    - Launch the SnapBridge app on your smartphone.
3. **Connect to the Camera**:
    - On the camera, go to **Wi-Fi Settings** and choose **Connect to Smart Device**.
    - The camera will display a unique SSID (network name) and password.
4. **Select the Camera's Wi-Fi Network on Your Phone**:
    - On your smartphone, go to the Wi-Fi settings and connect to the camera's network using the SSID and password provided by the camera.

5. **Confirm the Connection**:
    - After connecting, the SnapBridge app should automatically recognize the camera and establish a connection.

6. **Transfer Photos or Control the Camera**:
    - You can now use the SnapBridge app to transfer photos, remotely control the camera, or adjust settings.

2. Setting Up Bluetooth on the Nikon D7500

Bluetooth allows for a continuous connection between your camera and your smartphone or tablet. This is especially useful for automatic image transfers, geotagging, and remote control without using Wi-Fi.

Step 1: Enable Bluetooth on the Camera

1. **Press the Menu Button**:
    - Open the **Menu** and navigate to the **Setup Menu** (wrench icon).

2. **Select Bluetooth Settings**:
    - Scroll down to find **Bluetooth Settings**.

3. **Turn Bluetooth On**:
    - Set Bluetooth to **On** to allow the camera to connect to compatible devices.

Step 2: Pair the Camera with Your Smartphone Using Bluetooth

1. **Open the SnapBridge App**:
    - Launch the **SnapBridge** app on your smartphone if it's not already open.

2. **Enable Bluetooth on Your Phone**:
    - Make sure **Bluetooth** is enabled on your smartphone.

3. **Pair the Camera with Your Phone**:
    - The SnapBridge app will search for compatible devices. Once it finds the camera, follow the prompts to pair the two devices.

4. **Confirm Pairing**:
    - After pairing, you should see the camera's Bluetooth name listed in the app, confirming the connection.

5. **Use Bluetooth Features**:
    - Once paired, Bluetooth allows for features like automatic image transfer, location tagging, and remote shutter release (even when the phone's screen is off).

3. Transferring Photos Using Wi-Fi and Bluetooth

After setting up Wi-Fi and Bluetooth, you can easily transfer photos from your Nikon D7500 to your smartphone or tablet.

Using Wi-Fi for Image Transfer

1. **Open the SnapBridge App**:
    - Launch the **SnapBridge** app and make sure it's connected to the camera via Wi-Fi.

2. **Select Images for Transfer**:
    - In the app, browse through the images stored on the camera.
    - Select the photos or videos you want to transfer to your phone.

3. **Start the Transfer**:
    - Tap on the **Download** icon in the SnapBridge app to begin transferring the selected images to your phone or tablet.

Using Bluetooth for Automatic Transfers

1. **Automatic Transfer**:
    - With Bluetooth enabled, SnapBridge can automatically transfer photos to your smartphone after they're taken. Simply take a picture, and the app will handle the transfer in the background.

2. **Control Automatic Transfers**:
    - In the SnapBridge app, go to **Settings** and customize the automatic transfer settings, such as whether images are transferred only when you press the shutter or immediately after each shot.

4. Remote Camera Control via Wi-Fi and Bluetooth

The Nikon D7500 allows remote control via both Wi-Fi and Bluetooth. Here's how to do it:

Using Wi-Fi for Remote Control

1. **Launch the SnapBridge App**:
    - Open the SnapBridge app and connect to the camera via Wi-Fi.

2. **Enable Remote Photography**:
    - In the app, select the **Remote Photography** option to control the camera remotely.

3. **Adjust Camera Settings**:
    - Use the app to adjust settings like exposure, shutter speed, and aperture remotely.

4. **Take Photos Remotely**:
    - Once everything is set, tap the shutter button in the app to take a photo without touching the camera.

Using Bluetooth for Remote Control

1. **Activate Bluetooth**:
   - Ensure Bluetooth is on, and the camera is paired with your phone via the SnapBridge app.

2. **Remote Shutter**:
   - You can use Bluetooth to remotely trigger the camera's shutter, making it easier for self-portraits or group shots without needing a physical remote.

5. Tips for Using Wi-Fi and Bluetooth on the Nikon D7500

- **Battery Consumption**: Both Wi-Fi and Bluetooth can consume a lot of battery, especially when transferring images. Consider carrying spare batteries or using the camera's AC adapter when using these features extensively.

- **Wi-Fi Range**: The Wi-Fi connection is typically effective at a range of 10–15 meters, depending on obstacles like walls. Make sure you are within this range for a stable connection.

- **Bluetooth for Low Power**: If you just need a low-energy connection for transferring small files or geotagging, Bluetooth is more efficient and consumes less power compared to Wi-Fi.

- **Use SnapBridge for Auto Sync**: To ensure seamless photo transfer after each shot, use the SnapBridge app's automatic syncing feature, which works continuously in the background.

Setting up Wi-Fi and Bluetooth on the Nikon D7500 is an excellent way to streamline your workflow and enhance your photography experience. By enabling these features, you can quickly transfer photos, remotely control the camera, and share your images instantly. Whether you're a professional photographer or an enthusiast, using these wireless features makes it easy to connect your camera to your devices and access your images on the go.

9.2 Using SnapBridge for File Transfer

SnapBridge is a powerful app by Nikon that allows you to wirelessly transfer photos and videos from your Nikon D7500 camera to your smartphone or tablet. With SnapBridge, you can seamlessly transfer images, control your camera remotely, and manage your files, all while using the built-in Wi-Fi and Bluetooth features of the D7500.

Here's a detailed guide on how to use SnapBridge for file transfer

1. Setting Up SnapBridge on Your Smartphone

Before transferring files, you need to install and configure the **SnapBridge app** on your smartphone or tablet.

Step 1: Download and Install the SnapBridge App

1. **Download the App**:
   - **For iOS**: Go to the **App Store** and search for **Nikon SnapBridge**.
   - **For Android**: Go to **Google Play** and search for **Nikon SnapBridge**.

2. **Install the App**:
   - Tap the **Install** button and wait for the app to download and install.

Step 2: Create an Account (Optional)

1. **Open the SnapBridge App**:
   - Launch the app once it's installed on your smartphone.

2. **Create an Account (Optional)**:
   - You can choose to create a Nikon account for personalized features and syncing. If you prefer, you can skip this step and just proceed with the connection.

2. Connecting the Nikon D7500 to SnapBridge

Once the app is installed, you need to connect your Nikon D7500 to the SnapBridge app via **Wi-Fi** or **Bluetooth**.

Step 1: Turn On Wi-Fi and Bluetooth on the Camera

1. **Press the Menu Button** on your Nikon D7500.

2. **Go to the Setup Menu (Wrench Icon)**:
   - Scroll down and select **Wi-Fi** and **Bluetooth** to turn both settings on.

3. **Select "Connect to Smart Device"**:
   - The camera will start broadcasting its Wi-Fi signal. It will also display a network name (SSID) and password on the screen for pairing.

Step 2: Pair the Camera with the Smartphone

1. **Open the SnapBridge App**:
   - On your smartphone, open the SnapBridge app.

2. **Choose "Connect to Camera"**:
   - Tap on **Connect to Camera** in the app, and the app will search for nearby Nikon cameras.

3. **Select Your Camera**:
   - Select your **Nikon D7500** from the list of available cameras.

4. **Enter Wi-Fi Details (if prompted)**:
   - The app may ask you to enter the camera's Wi-Fi network details (SSID and password). Follow the on-screen prompts to complete the connection.

5. **Confirm the Connection**:
   - After successfully pairing the devices, the app will show that the camera is connected.

3. Transferring Files Using SnapBridge

With your Nikon D7500 connected to the SnapBridge app, you can now transfer images and videos to your smartphone or tablet.

Option 1: Auto Transfer of Images (Bluetooth + Wi-Fi)

SnapBridge can automatically transfer images to your smartphone after each shot. This is useful for continuous syncing, so you don't have to manually select files for transfer.

1. **Enable Auto Transfer**:
    - In the SnapBridge app, go to **Settings** and enable **Auto Transfer** to automatically sync images as soon as they are taken.

2. **Take Photos**:
    - When you capture images with your Nikon D7500, the app will automatically transfer the selected images to your phone, either through Bluetooth (for smaller files) or Wi-Fi (for larger files).

3. **View and Manage Transferred Files**:
    - Once the images are transferred, you can view, edit, or share them directly from the SnapBridge app.

Option 2: Manual File Transfer

If you want to manually select and transfer specific images, follow these steps:

1. **Open the SnapBridge App**:
    - Launch the SnapBridge app on your smartphone.

2. **Browse Camera Images**:
    - Tap **Camera Gallery** or **Images on Camera** to access the photos stored on the Nikon D7500.

3. **Select Files to Transfer**:
    - Browse through the gallery and select the images or videos you want to transfer.

4. **Initiate the Transfer**:
    - Tap **Download** or **Transfer** to begin transferring the selected files from the camera to your smartphone.

5. **Wait for Completion**:
    - Wait for the transfer process to complete. The time required will depend on the number and size of the files being transferred.

4. Transferring Videos Using SnapBridge

SnapBridge can also be used to transfer videos from your Nikon D7500, but keep in mind that large video files may require Wi-Fi for quicker transfer.

Step 1: Open the Camera's Video Gallery

- In the SnapBridge app, go to the **Camera Gallery** and select the **Videos** section to view all video files on the camera.

Step 2: Select Videos for Transfer

- Tap to select the videos you want to transfer to your phone.

Step 3: Transfer Videos

- After selecting, tap **Download** or **Transfer**, and wait for the video to be transferred. Larger videos may take longer, so ensure a stable Wi-Fi connection for faster speeds.

5. Remote Control and File Management Using SnapBridge

Beyond transferring files, SnapBridge allows you to remotely control your Nikon D7500 and manage your media files.

Using SnapBridge for Remote Photography

1. **Enable Remote Photography**:
   - In the SnapBridge app, select **Remote Photography** to take control of the camera's settings like exposure, aperture, and shutter speed.

2. **Capture Photos Remotely**:
   - Tap the shutter button in the app to take a photo remotely. This is ideal for self-portraits, group shots, or when the camera is mounted on a tripod.

Managing Files in the SnapBridge App

1. **Sort and Edit Files**:
   - In the SnapBridge app, you can sort photos by date, file type, or category.

2. **Delete Files**:
   - You can delete unwanted files directly from the app after reviewing them.

6. Tips for Using SnapBridge for File Transfer

- **Battery Life**: Keep an eye on your camera's and smartphone's battery when using SnapBridge, especially for continuous transfers. Both Bluetooth and Wi-Fi use power.

- **File Size**: Larger files like RAW images and videos might take longer to transfer. Use Wi-Fi for faster transfer speeds, particularly for videos.

- **Data Usage**: Be mindful of your mobile data usage, as transferring large files can consume significant data if not using a Wi-Fi network.

- **Automatic Sync Settings**: You can adjust the SnapBridge app settings to control how and when images are transferred. For example, choose to transfer only certain file types or limit transfers to when connected via Wi-Fi.

SnapBridge offers a seamless way to transfer photos and videos from your Nikon D7500 to your smartphone or tablet using both **Wi-Fi** and **Bluetooth**. Whether you prefer automatic transfers or manual selection, SnapBridge makes it easy to share your media and manage your files on the go. By following the steps above, you can quickly and efficiently use SnapBridge to enhance your photography experience.

9.3 Remote Shooting with a Smartphone

The Nikon D7500 offers the ability to control the camera remotely using your smartphone or tablet, which is ideal for capturing shots without physically touching the camera. This feature is especially useful for group photos, self-portraits, wildlife photography, or when the camera is mounted on a tripod. Using SnapBridge, Nikon's wireless connectivity app, you can access a range of camera functions, including remote shooting, via Wi-Fi or Bluetooth.

Here's a step-by-step guide on how to use your smartphone to remotely control the Nikon D7500 for shooting:

1. Setting Up the Connection

Before you can use remote shooting, you need to connect your Nikon D7500 to your smartphone via the **SnapBridge** app using Wi-Fi or Bluetooth.

Step 1: Download and Install the SnapBridge App

1. **For iOS**: Go to the **App Store** and search for **Nikon SnapBridge**.
2. **For Android**: Go to **Google Play** and search for **Nikon SnapBridge**.
3. **Install the App** on your smartphone.

Step 2: Enable Wi-Fi and Bluetooth on the Camera

1. **Press the Menu Button** on your Nikon D7500.
2. **Go to the Setup Menu** (Wrench Icon).
3. Select **Wi-Fi** and **Bluetooth**, and turn both settings **On**.
4. Choose **Connect to Smart Device**, and the camera will start broadcasting its Wi-Fi signal.

Step 3: Pair the Camera with Your Smartphone

1. **Open the SnapBridge App** on your smartphone.
2. Follow the on-screen prompts in the app to pair your camera. Select **Connect to Camera** in SnapBridge.
3. Enter the camera's Wi-Fi details (SSID and password) if prompted. Once connected, SnapBridge will indicate that your camera is ready for remote control.

2. Setting Up Remote Shooting

Once the camera is connected to your smartphone, you can begin using your phone to control the Nikon D7500 remotely.

Step 1: Launch the SnapBridge App

- Open the **SnapBridge** app on your smartphone.
- Ensure that the app is connected to your Nikon D7500 via Wi-Fi or Bluetooth.

Step 2: Enable Remote Photography Mode

1. In the SnapBridge app, look for the **Remote Photography** option.
2. Tap **Remote Photography** to enter the camera control mode.

Step 3: Adjust Camera Settings (Optional)

- **Adjust settings** such as exposure, aperture, shutter speed, and ISO directly from the SnapBridge app before taking the shot.
- You can also change the **autofocus mode**, **white balance**, and **image quality** settings via the app.

3. Taking Photos Remotely

With the camera connected and the remote photography mode activated, you can now capture images using your smartphone.

Step 1: Frame Your Shot

- **View the live feed** from your camera on your smartphone screen. This helps you frame the shot, adjust composition, and check the focus.

Step 2: Focus the Camera

- **Tap the focus area** on your smartphone screen where you want the camera to focus. The camera will automatically adjust focus on the selected area.

Step 3: Capture the Image

- **Press the shutter button** in the SnapBridge app to take the photo. You can press it once for a single shot or hold it down for continuous shooting (depending on the camera's settings).

4. Using Additional Features for Remote Control

Beyond basic shooting, SnapBridge offers several additional remote control features.

Live View Remote Control

- The **Live View** feature allows you to use your smartphone screen as the camera's viewfinder, enabling you to see what the camera sees in real-time. This is particularly useful when the camera is placed on a tripod or in a difficult-to-reach location.

Adjusting Settings in Real-Time

- You can adjust settings such as **ISO**, **shutter speed**, **aperture**, and **focus** from your smartphone screen in real-time.

Interval Timer Shooting

- Use your smartphone to set up **interval timer shooting**, ideal for capturing time-lapse sequences. You can set how often the camera takes photos and the number of shots.

Zoom Control

- If you are using a lens with zoom functionality, some third-party apps may allow you to remotely control zoom during shooting. However, this depends on the lens type and compatibility with SnapBridge.

5. Advanced Remote Control Features

In addition to basic shooting, SnapBridge provides several advanced features for controlling your Nikon D7500 remotely.

Time-Lapse Photography

- Using the **Interval Timer** feature, you can set up a time-lapse sequence from your smartphone. This is great for shooting scenes like sunsets or star trails.

Remote Video Recording

- While the remote control is primarily used for still images, SnapBridge also allows you to start and stop video recording remotely, although video control options are more limited than still photography.

GPS Tagging

- SnapBridge allows for **geotagging**, meaning the app can record the GPS location of the photos you take. This is automatically added to your images, making it easy to organize and track where your photos were taken.

6. Reviewing and Managing Photos Remotely

After taking a photo, you can immediately review and manage your images through SnapBridge.

Step 1: View Photos on Your Smartphone

- Browse through the captured images in the **Camera Roll** of the SnapBridge app. You can zoom in, delete, or mark images for future reference.

Step 2: Transfer Images to Your Smartphone

- If you want to save the images to your smartphone's gallery, simply select the photos in SnapBridge and transfer them using the **Download** button.

Step 3: Share Photos

- Once the images are transferred, you can directly share them on social media or with friends using the built-in sharing options in your smartphone's gallery.

7. Troubleshooting Remote Shooting with SnapBridge

If you encounter issues while using remote shooting, here are some common solutions:

Camera Not Connecting to SnapBridge

- Make sure that **Wi-Fi** and **Bluetooth** are turned on both in the camera and the SnapBridge app.
- Ensure that you are using the correct **SSID** and **password** when connecting.
- Restart the camera and the smartphone and try reconnecting.

Delayed Shutter Response

- If there is a delay when taking a photo, check the camera's **Wi-Fi connection strength**. Being too far from the camera can result in delays.
- Ensure your smartphone is connected to the camera's Wi-Fi network with a stable signal.

App Crashing or Freezing

- Ensure that you are using the latest version of the SnapBridge app. Update the app if necessary.
- Try restarting the app or reinstalling it if it continues to crash.

Remote shooting with your Nikon D7500 and a smartphone via SnapBridge is an excellent way to capture photos without physically touching the camera. Whether you're taking a group shot, capturing wildlife, or setting up a complex scene, SnapBridge makes it easy to control your camera remotely, adjust settings, and transfer images instantly. By following the steps outlined above, you can unlock the full potential of your Nikon D7500's remote shooting capabilities.

CHAPTER TEN
ACCESSORIES AND EXPANSION

10.1 Compatible Lenses

The Nikon D7500 is a versatile DSLR camera that supports a wide range of lenses, making it suitable for various photography styles. Here's an overview of compatible lenses categorized by type, along with some specific recommendations.

Types of Compatible Lenses

1. **DX Format Lenses**: These are designed specifically for Nikon's crop sensor cameras. They provide optimal performance on the D7500.

2. **FX Format Lenses**: Full-frame lenses can also be used on the D7500, but they will have a crop factor of approximately 1.5x, affecting the effective focal length.

3. **Third-Party Lenses**: Brands like Sigma and Tamron offer lenses that are compatible with the D7500, often providing excellent quality at competitive prices.

Recommended Lenses

Wide-Angle Lenses

- **Tamron 10-24mm f/3.5-4.5 Di II VC HLD**: Great for landscapes and architecture, this lens offers a wide field of view suitable for crop sensors (effective focal length of 15-36mm)

- **Nikon AF-S DX NIKKOR 10-24mm f/3.5-4.5G ED**: Another excellent choice for wide-angle shots, providing sharp images and minimal distortion

Standard Zoom Lenses

- **Nikon AF-S DX 16-80mm f/2.8-4E ED VR**: A versatile lens ideal for everyday photography, covering a useful focal range with good low-light performance.

- **Tamron 24-70mm f/2.8 Di VC USD G2**: Known for its quality and versatility, this lens is perfect for portraits and general photography.

Telephoto Lenses

- **Nikon AF-S NIKKOR 200-500mm f/5.6E ED VR**: Excellent for wildlife and sports photography, this lens provides a long reach with image stabilization.

- **Tamron 100-400mm f/4.5-6.3 Di VC USD**: A great option for those looking to capture distant subjects without sacrificing image quality.

Prime Lenses

- **Sigma 18-35mm f/1.8 DC HSM**: Highly regarded for its sharpness and low-light capabilities, making it ideal for both landscapes and portraits.

- **Nikon AF-S DX 35mm f/1.8G**: A lightweight prime lens that excels in low-light situations and offers a natural perspective.

Macro Lenses

- **Nikon AF-S DX 40mm f/2.8 Micro**: Perfect for macro photography, this lens is affordable and versatile, allowing close-up shots with excellent detail.

Lens Compatibility Considerations

When selecting lenses for the Nikon D7500:

- Ensure that the lens is compatible with the Nikon F mount.
- Look for CPU lenses (types G, E, and D) to utilize all camera features fully.
- Be aware of the crop factor when using FX lenses to understand their effective focal lengths better.

Using these guidelines will help you choose the right lenses to enhance your photography experience with the Nikon D7500.

10.2 External Flashes (Speedlights)

The Nikon D7500 is compatible with various external flashes (speedlights), allowing photographers to enhance their lighting options. Here's a summary of compatible speedlights and considerations for using them with the D7500.

Compatible Speedlights

Nikon Speedlights

1. **SB-5000**: Offers advanced features including radio control and excellent performance in various lighting conditions.
2. **SB-910**: Known for its reliability and versatility, it provides good battery life and consistent performance.
3. **SB-900**: While it is compatible, some users report limitations in controlling it through the camera's flash control menu, particularly regarding pre-flashes and settings adjustments
4. **SB-700**: A solid choice for general use, providing good power and features at a more affordable price.
5. **SB-600**: An older model but still effective for basic flash needs.

Third-Party Speedlights

1. **Godox V860II**: Highly recommended for its TTL support and built-in lithium battery, which offers longer usage times.
2. **Yongnuo YN685**: A budget-friendly option that supports TTL and has a decent range of features.
3. **Metz 52 AF-1**: This flash is noted for its compatibility with Nikon cameras, though some users have reported mixed experiences regarding functionality with the D7500

Considerations

- **TTL Compatibility**: Ensure that the flash supports i-TTL (intelligent Through The Lens) metering to take full advantage of the D7500's capabilities.
- **Firmware Updates**: Keeping both the camera and flash firmware updated can resolve compatibility issues and enhance performance
- **Control Limitations**: Some flashes, like the SB-900, may not allow full control via the camera menu, which can limit functionality in certain shooting scenarios

When selecting an external flash for the Nikon D7500, it's essential to consider both Nikon's own speedlights and reputable third-party options like Godox and Yongnuo. Each option has its strengths, so choose based on your specific photography needs and preferences.

10.3 Tripods and Stabilizers

When selecting tripods and stabilizers for the Nikon D7500, it's important to consider stability, weight, and versatility to enhance your photography experience. Here's an overview of suitable options based on the available search results.

Recommended Tripods

1. KamKorda Compact Advanced Tripod

- **Features**: This tripod is part of a kit that includes a camera bag and flash, making it a convenient option for photographers on the go. It is designed for stability and ease of use.
- **Use Case**: Ideal for general photography, especially in low-light conditions where stability is crucial

2. CR 125 Radiator Hose Tripod

- **Features**: Known for its wide base plate, this tripod provides excellent stability, making it suitable for various shooting scenarios.
- **Use Case**: A popular choice among Nikon D7500 users, particularly for outdoor photography or when using heavier lenses

3. MyMemory Tripods

- **Features**: MyMemory offers a variety of tripods specifically compatible with the Nikon D7500, ensuring a good fit and functionality.
- **Use Case**: These tripods cater to different needs, from lightweight travel options to more robust models for studio work

Stabilizers

1. Gimbals

- **Zhiyun Crane Series**: These gimbals are excellent for video stabilization, allowing for smooth footage even while moving.

- **DJI Ronin-S**: Another great option that provides advanced stabilization features, suitable for videographers looking to capture dynamic shots.

2. Monopods

- **Manfrotto XPRO Monopod**: Offers flexibility and portability while providing support for quick shots or video recording.
- **Benro Adventure Series Monopod**: Known for its sturdy build and lightweight design, ideal for travel and outdoor photography.

Considerations When Choosing Tripods and Stabilizers

- **Weight Capacity**: Ensure the tripod can support the weight of your Nikon D7500 and any attached lenses or accessories.
- **Height and Portability**: Consider your typical shooting environment; a lightweight and compact design is beneficial for travel.
- **Head Type**: Look for tripods with ball heads or pan-tilt heads based on your shooting style (e.g., landscape vs. portrait).

By selecting the right tripod or stabilizer, you can significantly improve your shooting experience with the Nikon D7500, ensuring stability and enhancing image quality in various conditions.

10.4 Battery Grip and Extra Batteries

For the Nikon D7500, battery grips and extra batteries are essential accessories that enhance shooting experience, especially for extended sessions. Here's a detailed overview of available options.

Battery Grips

1. Vello BG-N18 Battery Grip

- **Compatibility**: Specifically designed for the Nikon D7500.
- **Battery Type**: Holds one EN-EL15a battery.
- **Features**:
    - Vertical shutter release button for easier portrait shooting.
    - Non-slip rubberized grip for better handling.
    - Includes a 2.5mm shutter release cable.
    - 1/4"-20 tripod mounting socket.
- **Price**: Approximately $49

.2. Mcoplus BG-D7500 Vertical Battery Grip

- **Compatibility**: Designed for the Nikon D7500.
- **Battery Type**: Accepts one EN-EL15a or EN-EL15 battery.

- **Material**: ABS plastic, mimicking the texture of the camera body for a seamless feel

3. Generic MB-D7500 Battery Grip

- **Compatibility**: Fits Nikon D7500.
- **Battery Type**: Uses one EN-EL15a or EN-EL15 battery.
- **Note**: This grip does not support AA batteries and is made from durable ABS material

Extra Batteries

Nikon EN-EL15a Battery

- **Specifications**:
    - Type: Rechargeable Lithium-Ion.
    - Voltage: 7.0V DC.
    - Capacity: 1900mAh, providing approximately 950 shots per charge (CIPA rating).
- **Charging**: Can be charged using the Nikon MH-25a charger, sold separately.
- **Alternatives**: Generic versions of the EN-EL15a are available at lower prices, often providing good performance, though quality can vary. Brands like Wasabi and Patona are noted for their reliability in third-party batteries

Considerations

When using battery grips and extra batteries with the Nikon D7500:

- The Vello grip does not extend battery life; it merely relocates the battery from the camera to the grip, enhancing ergonomics
- Ensure that any third-party grip or battery is compatible with your specific shooting needs and quality expectations.

By utilizing these battery grips and additional batteries, photographers can significantly improve their shooting experience with the Nikon D7500, particularly during long shoots or when capturing vertical compositions.

CHAPTER ELEVEN
MAINTENANCE AND TROUBLESHOOTING

11.1 Cleaning the Camera and Lens

Cleaning your Nikon D7500 and its lenses is essential for maintaining image quality and ensuring the longevity of your equipment. Here's a comprehensive guide on how to clean both the camera body and lenses effectively.

Cleaning the Camera Body

1. Dust and Dirt Removal

- **Tools Needed**: Use a soft, lint-free microfiber cloth to wipe down the camera body. For stubborn dirt, a blower can help dislodge dust without scratching the surface.

- **Method**: Gently wipe the exterior surfaces, including buttons and grips, to remove fingerprints and smudges.

2. Sensor Cleaning

The sensor is delicate and should be handled with care. Here are the steps for cleaning it:

Automatic Cleaning

- Navigate to the **Setup Menu** on your camera.

- Select **Clean Image Sensor** and choose **Clean Now**. This feature uses vibrations to dislodge dust from the sensor surface

Manual Cleaning

If automatic cleaning does not suffice, follow these steps:

1. **Prepare the Camera**:
   - Charge your battery or connect an AC adapter to ensure reliable power.
   - Turn off the camera and remove the lens.

2. **Lock Mirror Up for Cleaning**:
   - Turn on the camera and navigate to **Lock Mirror Up for Cleaning** in the Setup Menu.
   - Press the shutter button to raise the mirror, exposing the sensor

3. **Inspect the Sensor**:
   - Use a bright light to check for dust or debris on the sensor surface.

4. **Clean with Care**:
   - Use a blower (not your mouth) to gently blow away dust particles.

- If necessary, use a clean sensor swab with appropriate cleaning solution for any stubborn spots. Avoid touching or wiping the sensor directly with anything other than designated cleaning tools

5. **Finish Up**:
   - Turn off the camera to lower the mirror back into position, then replace the lens or body cap.

Cleaning Lenses

1. Dust and Smudges

- **Tools Needed**: A microfiber cloth, lens brush, or blower.
- **Method**:
  - Start by using a blower to remove loose dust from the lens surface.
  - For smudges, use a microfiber cloth slightly dampened with lens cleaning solution or distilled water. Wipe in circular motions from the center outward.

2. Lens Elements

- Clean both front and rear elements of the lens carefully using similar techniques as above.
- Avoid using paper towels or rough fabrics that could scratch the lens coating.

Additional Tips

- Always work in a clean environment to minimize dust exposure.
- Perform regular checks of your equipment; clean as needed but avoid over-cleaning, which can lead to wear on sensitive components.
- If you are uncomfortable cleaning the sensor yourself, consider professional cleaning services.

By following these guidelines, you can keep your Nikon D7500 and its lenses in optimal condition, ensuring high-quality images and prolonged equipment life.

11.2 Updating Firmware

The Nikon D7500, like any camera, may encounter various issues during use. Here's a summary of common problems reported by users along with their potential solutions.

Common Problems and Solutions

1. Camera Freezing After Using Built-in Flash

- **Issue**: The camera may freeze after the second use of the built-in flash, requiring a restart to function again.
- **Solution**: This could be a firmware issue. Ensure your camera firmware is updated to the latest version. If the problem persists, consider using an external flash to avoid triggering the built-in flash.

2. Camera Not Turning On

- **Issue**: The camera may become unresponsive or fail to turn on.
- **Solutions**:
  - Remove the battery for several minutes or leave it out for days to reset internal settings.
  - Check if the battery is fully charged and functioning properly. If possible, test with another battery.
  - Ensure that no lens is mounted when testing if the camera powers on.

3. ERR Message Displayed

- **Issue**: The camera displays an ERR message in modes other than Manual.
- **Solutions**:
  - Clean the lens contacts with a microfiber cloth dipped in isopropyl alcohol to ensure good electrical contact.
  - Check for any issues with the aperture lever if using non-CPU lenses.
  - If the problem continues, consider resetting the camera settings to factory defaults.

4. Focus Issues

- **Issue**: Consistently blurry images or difficulty focusing, even with multiple lenses.
- **Solutions**:
  - Ensure that autofocus is enabled and set to AF-S mode for single shots.
  - Check if the focus point is correctly selected and adjust if necessary.
  - If autofocus issues persist across multiple lenses, it may indicate a problem with the autofocus sensor in the camera body, requiring professional servicing.

5. Slow Response to Shutter Release

- **Issue**: The camera takes time to respond when pressing the shutter button.
- **Solution**: Turn off any exposure delay modes in the custom settings menu, which can slow down response times.

6. Memory Card Issues

- **Issue**: The camera fails to recognize the memory card or shows "Card Error."
- **Solutions**:
  - Ensure that the memory card is properly formatted and compatible with the D7500.
  - Try using a different memory card to rule out card failure.
  - Clean the card contacts and check for physical damage.

7. Dark Viewfinder or Out of Focus

- **Issue**: The viewfinder appears dark or out of focus.
- **Solutions**:
    - Adjust the diopter control located next to the viewfinder until you achieve a clear image.
    - Ensure that a fully charged battery is inserted.

8. Noise in Photos

- **Issue**: Bright spots, random bright pixels, or lines appear in images.
- **Solutions**:
    - Lower ISO sensitivity settings as high ISO can introduce noise.
    - Use noise reduction features available in-camera or during post-processing.

By addressing these common issues with their respective solutions, Nikon D7500 users can enhance their shooting experience and resolve many operational challenges effectively. If problems persist despite troubleshooting, seeking professional repair services may be necessary.

11.3 Common Problems and Solutions

The Nikon D7500, while a robust camera, can experience various issues that may affect its performance. Here's a compilation of common problems users face along with their potential solutions based on the search results.

Common Problems and Solutions

1. Camera Freezing After Using Built-in Flash

- **Issue**: The camera may freeze after using the built-in flash, requiring a restart to regain functionality.
- **Solution**: This is likely a firmware issue. Users should ensure their firmware is updated to the latest version. If the problem persists, consider using an external flash instead of the built-in one to avoid triggering this issue repeatedly **2. Camera Not Turning On**
- **Issue**: The camera fails to power on.
- **Solutions**:
    - Remove and reinsert the battery, ensuring it is fully charged.
    - If using an AC adapter, disconnect and reconnect it
    - Leave the camera without a battery for several days to reset internal settings, then reinsert a charged battery

3. ERR Message Displayed

- **Issue**: The camera displays an ERR message in various modes.

- **Solutions**:
    - Clean the lens contacts with a microfiber cloth dipped in isopropyl alcohol to ensure proper electrical contact.
    - Check for issues with the aperture lever if using non-CPU lenses.
    - Reset the camera settings to factory defaults if necessary

4. Focus Issues

- **Issue**: Consistently blurry images or difficulty focusing.
- **Solutions**:
    - Ensure autofocus is enabled and set to AF-S mode for single shots.
    - Check if the focus point is correctly selected and adjust if necessary.
    - If autofocus issues persist across multiple lenses, it may indicate a problem with the autofocus sensor in the camera body

5. Slow Response to Shutter Release

- **Issue**: The camera takes time to respond when pressing the shutter button.
- **Solution**: Turn off any exposure delay modes in the custom settings menu, which can slow down response times.

6. Memory Card Issues

- **Issue**: The camera fails to recognize the memory card or shows "Card Error."
- **Solutions**:
    - Ensure that the memory card is properly formatted and compatible with the D7500.
    - Try using a different memory card to rule out card failure.
    - Clean the card contacts and check for physical damage.

7. Dark or Out-of-Focus Viewfinder

- **Issue**: The viewfinder appears dark or out of focus.
- **Solutions**:
    - Adjust the diopter control next to the viewfinder until you achieve a clear image.
    - Insert a fully charged battery as low power can affect viewfinder brightness.

8. Noise in Photos

- **Issue**: Bright spots or lines appear in images.
- **Solutions**:
    - Lower ISO sensitivity settings as high ISO can introduce noise.

- Use noise reduction features available in-camera or during post-processing
- By addressing these common issues with their respective solutions, Nikon D7500 users can enhance their shooting experience and resolve many operational challenges effectively. If problems persist despite troubleshooting, seeking professional repair services may be necessary.

11.4 Resetting to Default Settings

Resetting your Nikon D7500 to its default settings can help resolve various issues or simply restore the camera to its original configuration. Here's how to perform a reset using both the two-button method and the menu options.

Resetting to Default Settings

1. Two-Button Reset Method

This method quickly resets most camera settings to their factory defaults.

- **Steps**:
    1. Locate the **W (Z)** and **E** buttons on your camera, which are marked with green dots.
    2. Press and hold both buttons simultaneously for more than two seconds.
    3. The control panel will briefly turn off, indicating that the reset is complete.

2. Menu Reset Method

If you prefer a more detailed reset or if the two-button method does not suit your needs, you can use the camera menu.

- **Steps**:
    1. Turn on your camera and press the **Menu** button.
    2. Navigate to the **Setup Menu** (the spanner icon).
    3. Scroll down and select **Reset All Settings**.
    4. Confirm your selection by choosing **Yes** when prompted.

3. Reset Specific Settings

You can also reset specific settings in different menus:

- **Photo Shooting Menu**:
    - Go to the Photo Shooting Menu, highlight **Reset Photo Shooting Menu**, and confirm.
- **Movie Shooting Menu**:
    - Access the Movie Shooting Menu, highlight **Reset Movie Shooting Menu**, and confirm.

- **Custom Settings Menu**:
    - Navigate to the Custom Settings Menu, highlight **Reset Custom Settings**, and confirm.

Important Notes

- The two-button reset restores settings related to shooting modes, ISO sensitivity, white balance, autofocus settings, and more.
- Some settings, like language and time zone, are not affected by these resets.
- It's advisable to save your current settings using the **Save/Load Settings** option in the Setup Menu before performing a reset if you want to retain specific configurations for future use

By following these steps, you can easily reset your Nikon D7500 to its default settings, helping to resolve any operational issues or prepare the camera for a new user.

CHAPTER TWELVE
APPENDICES

12.1 Technical Specifications

The Nikon D7500 is a high-performance DSLR camera that features an array of advanced specifications suited for both amateur and professional photographers. Below are the key technical specifications of the Nikon D7500:

General

- **Type**: Digital Single-Lens Reflex (DSLR)
- **Lens Mount**: Nikon F-mount (compatible with AF-S and AF-I lenses)
- **Image Sensor**:
  - **Type**: CMOS (APS-C size, DX-format)
  - **Size**: 23.5 x 15.7 mm
  - **Effective Pixels**: 20.9 megapixels
  - **Sensor Cleaning**: Image Sensor Cleaning (automatically and manually)

Image Processing

- **Processor**: Expeed 5 Image Processor
- **ISO Sensitivity**:
  - **Standard**: 100 to 51,200 (expandable to 50 to 1,640,000)
  - **Auto ISO**: Yes, with customizable limits

Autofocus System

- **Autofocus (AF) Type**: Phase Detection AF with 51 focus points
- **AF Points**: 51 AF points (15 cross-type points)
- **Focus Modes**:
  - **AF-S** (Single-servo AF)
  - **AF-C** (Continuous-servo AF)
  - **Manual Focus** (MF)
- **AF Detection Range**: -3 to +19 EV (ISO 100, 20°C/68°F)

Viewfinder and Display

- **Viewfinder Type**: Optical pentaprism viewfinder with 100% frame coverage
- **Viewfinder Magnification**: 0.94x

- **LCD Monitor**:
  - **Type**: 3.2-inch Vari-angle TFT touchscreen
  - **Resolution**: 922,000 dots
  - **Display Features**:
    - Touchscreen controls for focus, shutter release, and settings adjustments
    - Anti-reflection coating
    - 170° viewing angle

Shutter and Shooting Performance

- **Shutter Speed**:
  - **Range**: 1/8000 to 30 seconds
  - **Bulb Mode**: Yes
  - **Flash Sync Speed**: 1/250 sec
- **Continuous Shooting Speed**: 8 fps (frames per second)
- **Buffer**: 50 JPEGs or 18 RAW files at 8 fps (up to the camera's buffer limit)

Video Capabilities

- **Video Resolution**:
  - **4K UHD (3840 x 2160)** at 30p/25p/24p
  - **Full HD (1920 x 1080)** at 60p/50p/30p/25p/24p
  - **HD (1280 x 720)** at 120p for slow-motion recording
- **Audio**:
  - **Built-in Stereo Microphone**
  - **External Microphone Input** (3.5mm jack)
- **Time-Lapse**: Yes (in-camera processing)
- **Video Output**: HDMI Type C

Storage and Media

- **Media Type**:
  - **1 x SD/SDHC/SDXC card slot**
  - **Supports UHS-I memory cards**
- **File Formats**:
  - **Image**: JPEG, RAW (NEF), TIFF (via third-party software)

- o **Video**: MOV, MP4 (H.264/MPEG-4 AVC)

Connectivity

- **Wireless Connectivity**:
  - o **Wi-Fi**: Built-in
  - o **Bluetooth**: Built-in (Bluetooth Low Energy)
  - o **NFC**: No
- **GPS**: Via external GPS unit (not built-in)
- **HDMI Output**: Yes (Type C)
- **USB**: USB 2.0 (Micro-B)

Power Supply

- **Battery**:
  - o **Type**: EN-EL15a rechargeable Li-ion battery
  - o **Battery Life**: Approx. 950 shots (CIPA standard)
- **Battery Charging**: External charger (MH-25a)

Physical Specifications

- **Dimensions**: 135.5 x 104 x 72.5 mm (5.34 x 4.09 x 2.85 in)
- **Weight**: Approx. 720 g (1.59 lbs) with battery and memory card
- **Body**: Magnesium alloy with weather-sealing for durability

Additional Features

- **Dual SD Card Slot**: No (single SD card slot)
- **Flash**:
  - o Built-in pop-up flash (guide number 12m at ISO 100)
  - o **Flash Sync Speed**: 1/250 sec
  - o **Hot Shoe**: Yes (for external flashes)
- **Exposure Modes**:
  - o Program (P), Shutter-priority (S), Aperture-priority (A), Manual (M)
  - o Scene modes, Special effects modes, and Automatic modes
- **Metering System**:
  - o 3D Color Matrix Metering III
  - o Center-weighted, Spot metering

- o Exposure Compensation: ±5 EV
- **Self-Timer**: 2, 5, 10, or 20 seconds
- **In-Camera Processing**: RAW processing, cropping, red-eye correction, image rotation, etc.

Other Key Features

- **Touchscreen Interface**: Yes, for touch-to-focus and other controls
- **Weather-Sealing**: Yes, for protection against dust and moisture
- **Built-in Intervalometer**: For time-lapse photography
- **Focus Peaking**: Available in live view for manual focusing

The Nikon D7500 offers a great balance of performance, image quality, and advanced features, making it an excellent choice for both hobbyists and more advanced photographers. With a powerful 20.9 MP sensor, fast autofocus, high-speed continuous shooting, and versatile video capabilities, it is equipped to handle a wide range of photographic and video challenges. The camera's robust build and wireless connectivity options also provide flexibility in both studio and field work.

12.2 Glossary of Terms

Here is a glossary of common photography and camera-related terms you might encounter while using the **Nikon D7500**:

A

- **Aperture**: The opening in a lens through which light passes to enter the camera. It is expressed as an f-number (e.g., f/2.8, f/4). A lower f-number means a wider aperture, allowing more light to reach the sensor.
- **AF (Autofocus)**: A system that automatically adjusts the camera's lens to focus on the subject.
- **AF-S (Autofocus-Single)**: A focus mode where the camera focuses once when the shutter button is pressed halfway.
- **AF-C (Autofocus-Continuous)**: A focus mode where the camera continuously adjusts focus on moving subjects.
- **Anti-Distortion Shutter**: A type of electronic shutter used to reduce distortions in high-speed photography, especially with fast-moving subjects.

B

- **Bluetooth**: A wireless technology that allows the Nikon D7500 to connect to other devices (like smartphones) for transferring files or remote control.
- **Burst Mode**: A shooting mode that allows you to capture a series of images in rapid succession.

C

- **CMOS (Complementary Metal-Oxide-Semiconductor)**: A type of image sensor used in cameras. CMOS sensors are known for their low power consumption and high-quality images.

- **CIPA (Camera & Imaging Products Association)**: An organization that standardizes camera battery life testing. CIPA battery life refers to the number of shots a camera can take on a full charge under normal conditions.
- **Continuous Shooting**: A mode that allows the camera to take multiple pictures in quick succession by holding down the shutter button.

D

- **Depth of Field (DOF)**: The range of distance in a photo that appears sharp. A shallow depth of field has a small area in focus, while a deep depth of field keeps most of the image in focus.
- **DX Format**: A sensor size format used in Nikon cameras. It is smaller than the full-frame sensor (FX format) but still delivers high-quality images.

E

- **EV (Exposure Value)**: A measure of the exposure in a photo, determined by the aperture, shutter speed, and ISO settings. Adjusting the EV helps control how light or dark an image appears.
- **Expeed 5**: Nikon's proprietary image processor, providing fast processing speeds, high-quality images, and video capabilities.

F

- **Focal Length**: The distance between the lens and the camera sensor when the subject is in focus, typically measured in millimeters (mm). It influences the angle of view and magnification of the subject.
- **Frame Rate**: The number of frames per second (fps) captured during video recording. Higher frame rates allow for smoother video and slow-motion effects.

G

- **GPS**: Global Positioning System. Some cameras (with an external GPS unit) can embed location data into photos, providing geotags for reference.
- **Guide Number**: A measure of the power of a flash. It is used to determine the flash range based on the aperture and ISO settings.

H

- **HDR (High Dynamic Range)**: A technique used to create images with a greater range of brightness levels, often resulting in more vivid and detailed images, especially in high-contrast scenes.
- **Hot Shoe**: A mount on top of the camera for attaching external accessories, such as a flash or microphone.

I

- **ISO**: The sensitivity of the camera's sensor to light. Higher ISO values allow shooting in low light, but can introduce noise (graininess) in the image.

- **Interval Timer**: A feature that automatically takes photos at set intervals, useful for time-lapse photography.

L

- **Live View**: A camera mode that displays the image captured by the sensor in real time on the LCD screen, allowing you to compose and focus without looking through the viewfinder.
- **Lens Mount**: The part of the camera that holds the lens in place. The Nikon D7500 uses the Nikon F-mount.

M

- **Manual Mode**: A shooting mode where you control all camera settings, including aperture, shutter speed, and ISO, giving you full creative control over the exposure.
- **Metering Modes**: Different methods used by the camera to determine the exposure, based on the light levels in the scene. Common modes include Matrix, Center-weighted, and Spot metering.

N

- **Nikon F-Mount**: The lens mount system used by Nikon DSLR cameras, compatible with a wide variety of Nikon lenses.
- **Nikon SnapBridge**: Nikon's app that allows for wireless connection between the camera and smartphones for file transfers and remote control.

P

- **P Mode (Program Mode)**: A shooting mode where the camera automatically selects the aperture and shutter speed, but allows you to adjust other settings like ISO.
- **Pixel**: The smallest unit of a digital image. More pixels typically result in higher image resolution.

R

- **RAW**: A file format that captures all of the data from the camera's sensor without any processing or compression. RAW files are larger but provide more flexibility in post-processing.

S

- **Shutter Speed**: The length of time the camera's shutter remains open to expose the sensor to light. Faster shutter speeds (e.g., 1/1000 sec) freeze motion, while slower speeds (e.g., 1/30 sec) create motion blur.
- **Spot Metering**: A metering mode that measures the light in a small area of the frame, often used for highly specific exposures (e.g., exposing for a subject in a bright environment).

T

- **Time-Lapse**: A technique where a series of photos are taken at regular intervals and played back at a faster speed, showing the passage of time.

- **Touchscreen**: A screen that allows you to interact with the camera's interface by touching the screen, useful for focusing, adjusting settings, and navigating menus.

V

- **Viewfinder**: The optical component that allows you to compose and focus your shots by looking through the lens. The Nikon D7500 has an optical pentaprism viewfinder.
- **Video Resolution**: The quality of video captured by the camera, usually expressed in terms of pixel resolution (e.g., 4K or 1080p).

W

- **Wi-Fi**: Wireless technology that allows the camera to connect to other devices for transferring photos or remote control. The Nikon D7500 supports Wi-Fi for connectivity.

Z

- **Zoom Lens**: A lens with a variable focal length, allowing you to zoom in and out on a subject without changing the lens.
- **Zero-Latency**: A term used to describe a camera's ability to capture images or video without any perceptible delay in response.

This glossary should help clarify many of the terms you'll encounter while using the Nikon D7500, making it easier to understand its features and settings!

THANK YOU FOR READING